BROTHER TO THE OX

The Autobiography of a Farm Labourer

Fred Kitchen

LITTLE TOLLER BOOKS

This paperback edition published in 2015 by
Little Toller Books
Lower Dairy, Toller Fratrum, Dorset

First published in 1940 by J.M. Dent & Sons

ISBN 978-1-908213-31-0

Text © The Estate of Fred Kitchen 2015
Introduction © Ian McMillan 2015
Photographs © Museum of English Rural Life 2015

We have made every effort to trace the copyright holders;
in the event of an inadvertent omission or error
please notify Little Toller Books.

Typeset in Monotype Sabon by Little Toller Books
Printed in Spain by GraphyCems, Navarra

All papers used by Little Toller Books
are natural, recyclable products made from
wood grown in sustainable, well-managed forests

A CIP catalogue record for this book is available
from the British Library

1 3 5 7 9 8 6 4 2

CONTENTS

INTRODUCTION

Ian McMillan

O<small>N SUNDAY AFTERNOONS</small> in the mid-1960s my dad would reverse his old blue Zephyr Six achingly slowly out of the cluttered garage and we'd go on what he called his 'Sunday afternoon run', although, to be honest, it was more of a trundle, through the kind of semi-rural West Riding landscapes captured so vividly and simply by Fred Kitchen in *Brother to the Ox*, first published in 1940.

We'd go down through Darfield on the A635, the old salt route from Cheshire to Leeds, past the narrow road to Houghton Main pit, the wheels turning as a shift came up or went down; up through Great Houghton past the Old Hall to Houghton Woods, down the road to Clayton where we often had to wait, the engine throbbing, as a herd of cattle wandered slowly around us like sluggish water passing a blue boulder in a stream. Behind us the Home Coal man's wagon waited too, the driver's fingers hovering over the horn. In the distance the pit bus turned out of Dearne Valley Drift, the gears crunching.

I didn't realise it at the time, but we were moving through a fieldscape and a pitscape that were on the cusp of disappearing for ever. The bloke at the back of the herd of cattle, lazily and expertly driving them along with a stick, was wearing a cap that had probably seen service since the war, or a war, and his trousers were held up with mucky string that he would have called a band. D.H. Lawrence would have recognised the physical, cultural and economic contours: the agricultural land on which the coal mines had been plonked like toys, the fields below which miners worked, sometimes so near the surface that you could hear them shouting, hear their machines; the big houses that dotted the area, home for mine-owners before Nationalisation, where the light was somehow different.

Fred Kitchen's book, like so many published around that time, gives us a glimpse into a world that was slipping away even when he wrote it in 1940. *Brother to the Ox* has been called 'anti-pastoral' because it doesn't romanticise the experience of working in the countryside and it's written in a kind of plain English that only creaks when he attempts to solder a bit of poetry to the sentences, which isn't often. It's the story of what some might call a small life, but it was a life that encompassed huge changes in what had hitherto been a settled existence, where the sun rose and the sun set and nothing much disturbed the day's still waters; the book is a vivid map of country we've forgotten how to get to, and now we never can. I first came across the book in my local library in a 1980s reprint; my dad borrowed it because he liked books about the countryside, although afterwards he told Mrs Dove that 'there wasn't enough fishing in it'. She shook her head. She knew the book was a gem. We're lucky it saw the light of day at all, because he sent it as a handwritten manuscript to the publishers; that's appropriate because the book has the fingerprint of authenticity, the rough music of the speaking voice rendered on the page.

Fred Kitchen was born in Edwinstowe in the heart of Sherwood Forest in 1890; he enjoyed school although he wasn't there for very long and he writes that the schoolmistress '. . . taught me to love and reverence good literature . . . life has been made rich because when ploughing up a nest of field-mice I could recite Robert Burns's "Ode to a Fieldmouse".' A theme throughout the book is the power of words to cleanse the human soul. Young Fred soon found himself working in the fields doing backbreaking toil. Here's a couple of paragraphs where he describes, in his matter-of-fact style, a working routine that would have killed me:

> 'We got up at five o'clock every morning, excepting Sunday, and then we laid an hour longer. I cleaned out the stable while George fed and watered the horses. Then I went to the cowshed and milked four cows – dairying was only a sideline in those days, beef and barley being the main products

– and took the milk into the house on the stroke of six. Breakfast was at six prompt. If I went in at three minutes past, the missus would say 'Tha wants to sharpen thi sen up in a mornin'; ere tha's bin an hour a-milkin four cows, an' corves awaiting for their parridge.'

I learned to have my breakfast with one eye on the calf-porridge. I had fat boiled bacon, with a basin of milk, for breakfast, and had never got very far into it before the missus would jerk the calf-porridge off the fire, saying 'ere, ma lad, just nip wi this afore it gets cowd. Ye can finish ateing when ye come back.'

There, in a few sentences, you have the essence of Fred Kitchen's style, a style without visible scaffolding; H.E. Bates said that he 'writes as the grass grows' and that's true. Here are short sentences that Ernest Hemingway would have coveted and here is a representation of dialect that doesn't patronise or render comic. And the prose moves along quickly, like Fred does. One minute he's in bed and within a few words he's trying to eat his fat boiled bacon before he has to set off again.

The book describes Fred's work on the soil and also how the shifting industrial times meant that it wasn't long before the railways arrived, or as Fred puts it, 'Then a loco came, fussing and snorting like some prehistoric monster, scattering the sheep and cattle from their grazing. It brought behind it engine sheds and fitting-shops, so that the miller's field, which had once been a sanctuary for birds, rang all day with a clatter and bang of hammers and the snorting of steam engines.' This led to Fred leaving the fields and going to work on the rails (amazingly, still only fifteen years old), still looking for the literary man in everyone: 'In that motley crew I have heard decrepit old navvies, lost to the world in filth and rags, declaim on the beauties of Shakespeare or verses of some great poet.'

He leaves the railways and goes back to the land as a 'shepherd lad' and meets the woman who will become his wife and because he needs to make a better living he goes to work at the coal mine: 'I had a great notion of getting work at the new pit that was being sunk at Little Norwood, for I was now nineteen, and it seemed a great age, and if I was to make a fortune and win Helen I had better get where I could addle some brass.'

The mines and the railways are perhaps spoiling the rural, almost feudal, idyll of his life, although there's a new idyll in his marriage to Helen as he sits reading Dickens to her as she sews. Sadly, Helen takes ill and dies and Kitchen memorably describes himself as 'finished with schemes and castles . . . drifted along like a ship that had lost its rudder.'

The story ends happily, though, when he marries Elizabeth: 'She can quote Shakespeare, chapter and verse, and turns out excellent crumpets, which is all I now ask of life.' Our Sunday afternoon runs would often end with tea at Grandma's, who wasn't my real grandma, and whose coconut cakes tasted like they were made of stuff you might make pit helmets out of.

Fred attends a local W.E.A course and is encouraged by the tutor and Elizabeth to write his story down. In just a few years he's gone from being a boy to a man, and now he can escape from being one of Thomas Gray's mute inglorious Miltons: 'I thought a bit, and I thought a bit; for I couldn't see how anyone would be interested in a farmer joskin, and then I settled down in my spare time to write my story. And this is it. I hope you like it.'

And I hope you do too.

Ian McMillan
Darfield, 2015

One

EARLY PASTURES

I WAS BORN AT EDWINSTOWE in Sherwood Forest, but my parents leaving that place soon after my entry into it, and going to live in Yorkshire, I cannot say much about my birthplace. I will set in a little further along, when my father was a cowman getting seventeen shillings a week, free house and garden, and a quart of new milk each day. That was the regular rate of pay in those days, and, in spite of index figures and all the Board of Trade likes to say about it, seventeen shillings went as far as does two pounds in these days. We lacked nothing on seventeen shillings a week in those days, and that's more than we can say today on thirty-six shillings or two pounds.

We lived on a nobleman's estate in South Yorkshire, or, to give it its proper name, the West Riding. It's those collier chaps who started calling it South Yorkshire. Our house was one of several situated in a large park of over three hundred acres. This was the playing field for some half-dozen children, and was shut in from the outer world by a high stone wall. We used to climb atop of the wall in summertime to watch the wagonettes and four-in-hands go driving by to the Abbey. I used to think what a busy place was the world over the park wall, and how well off were the trippers who went riding past and threw pennies away for little lads to scramble after in the long grass. But I liked best the long avenues of tall chestnuts and wide spread beeches. Here scores of rabbits went flippity-flop, flippity-flop across the grass ridings, or hopped lazily into the bracken when we approached. Herds of fallow-deer fed on the rough grass, or hid among the bracken with their heads stuck up so that they looked like a crowd of heads moving on top of the bracken without any bodies attached. The cottages and buildings were enclosed from the park by a ring fence of iron railings; through these railings we used to hold out crusts of bread or apples, trying to coax the deer to eat out of our hands. We could never tempt the timid does and fawns, but sometimes a wide-antlered stag would step up jauntily. He would be cautious too, his bright eyes staring hard at a row of fists thrust through the railings. Then his long neck would reach out, while his nostrils sniffed and quivered as he stepped an inch nearer. When he had got the crust or apple, away he would bounce like a big india rubber ball, and it would take weeks of coaxing before he would stay and eat out of our hands. The does were lovely soft-eyed creatures, but we could never get them to come up to the railings. The spotted ones were the loveliest, with light and dark brown markings; the white ones being of a dull white, and the black ones half brown.

All around the park stretched miles and miles of woodland, with a long, winding carriage drive leading down to the House, bordered with clipped yews, box and laurel bushes. Here we played hide and seek or Indians. It was a rare place for playing Indians, and we prowled about under the larch plantation. It was always dark under the larch trees, and though the plantation was only a small one, it gave us the idea of a great dark forest.

I roamed the woods for miles in search of birds' nests. The thrushes and blackies were easily found, every bush along the carriage drive owned a blackie or a thrush. It was the finches and tits that required searching for, and many a hiding I got for going home with my clothes torn through shinning up trees after birds' nests. Often I took my school mate, who lived next door, with me, but I liked nothing better than to go exploring the woods on my own.

You can never know, unless you start very early on in life, the joys and thrills of exploring the woods. I began this some time before I could make out difficult words like 'Trespassers' and 'Prosecuted', and by the time I had come to understand such long words the woods had claimed me as their own. It was a paradise for birds, being an out-o'-way sort of place, and by the time I was ten years old I knew the names and had a collection of over twenty different kinds of birds' eggs. These I kept in empty cigar boxes, begged off the estate steward. I even had a pheasant egg, and that was a serious offence.

I learned most of my woodcraft from the old mole-catcher. He was a little wisened, dried up man, and while supposed to be catching moles he wasn't above picking up a rabbit, or even partridge or pheasant eggs if the coast was clear. For that reason he was the sworn enemy of the game keepers, and because I had private reasons for not liking the keepers I liked the old mole-catcher. He taught me how to set a 'snickle' in a rabbit run, and how to tickle trout as they floated under the bank in the beck. I was never lucky enough to 'snickle' a rabbit, and the only time I caught a trout I fell into the beck with excitement. I took the trout home, expecting great praise for my prowess; all I got was an ash-plant across my sopping wet trousers, and I was sent to bed. I had committed a serious offence, though I was too young to know it, and as 'ashing a lad's behind' was the recognised form of punishment, and ash-plants grew in plenty, dad spoiled his nicely dried ash-plant of ever becoming useful as a walking stick.

Mind you, although he was strict, he was not more so than most dads. On an estate of not more than thirty houses of any kind, where his lordship is personally acquainted with every member of the community, where the chaplain or the school-ma'am may drop in any minute, parents had to be strict. Respectable was everything, but in spite of being brought up respectable, my fondness for prowling about in the woods was always getting me into hot water, and generally I needed hot water by the time I got home. I was a chubby little lad, and used to be dressed in corduroy knee breeches and a jersey – a woollen jersey for birds' nesting and scrawming through the bushes. I hated the sight of it, and used to hide it under a bush while I went exploring. Sometimes I forgot to call for it coming home, and sometimes I forgot where it was hidden, but the result was about the same. If my jersey was kept clean, my shirt wasn't, so I got tanned.

When I was ten I got the notion that there must be an end to this

particular wood somewhere; before then I had supposed it just went on
and on and there wasn't a place where there was no more wood. So, along
with the lad next door, I set out to investigate. We left my three sisters
gathering bluebells in the willow-garth, and entered the big wood. There
were lots of things to tempt a lad to enter the big wood besides the notice
stuck on the fir tree just inside the little hunting-gate. There was another
notice, too, on the middle riding, but as I never used either the gate or the
riding it didn't concern me what it said on the noticeboard. I always got a
creepy sort of feeling when prowling among the hazels and brambles and
bracken. Not scared though; a sort of 'churchy' feeling, like as if you must
tread softly and talk in whispers. The tall, straight-grained oaks, with arms
outstretched, seemed to challenge all comers to beware of trees passing;
while the beech trees, with arms twisted into fantastic shapes, looked like
big blue dragons. Some of the boughs touched the ground, and you saw the
loops of the dragon's back half-hidden in the ferns. There were elm and ash
too, but they didn't seem quite so important as the oak and beech, while
the lonely yew trees never seemed to have anything to do with the others.
When I was a small boy I thought it was the tall trees that made the wind
blow. On dark winter nights, when the wind howled through the woods, I
imagined the oak and the beech struggling with each other for the mastery
of the forest. And that was how the beech came to have his arms all twisted
and twirled.

It was a Saturday morning in early summer, and I was full of Captain
Marryat's *Settlers in Canada*. We were reading the story at school, and it
gave me a longing for adventure. The big wood was the nearest thing I
could get in place of the real Canadian forest. Whether I expected to meet
any Red Indians, or perhaps old Malachi Bone, or Martin the trapper, I
don't remember. All I remember now is trailing a little lad, a year younger
than myself, through brambles and fern, crawling under bushy hazels,
until our clothes were torn.

We felt lost. It was a delightful feeling for me, being not quite sure of
my whereabouts, and I whispered to my friend that we might meet an
adventure anywhere here about. We had left the badger holes, which was

the farthest extent of my wanderings until now, far behind. We threw stones at squirrels as they scampered up the tree-trunks, and disturbed pheasants that were deep i' sitting. All at once the bush wood ended and we stepped into a clearing.

I stared open-mouthed, for there, in front of us, were a party of Indians, with wigwams and all complete. Before we had time to dart back into the bushes a black-faced man standing in the doorway saw us and shouted out. Then the other men, who were building a pile of logs, came towards us and asked: 'What's you young shavers doin' 'ere?'

I mumbled something in reply, for I was scared – they looked so fierce. It was the first time I had seen the charcoal-burners at work, and though I pretended to be disappointed that they were not Red Indians I was well scared for the moment, breaking in on them in that way. It was interesting, however, watching the charcoal-burners at work, and I often went after that first visit. What they did with all the charcoal I'm not sure, but they used to say when I asked them that 'it were for makin' gunpowder for ta shoot the Boors!'

The cordwood was thick logs of about six feet in length. These were reared on end in shape of a pyramid, and then covered down with turf and soil. It was supposed to be highly skilled work, building the pile so as to regulate the draught to burn the logs off into charcoal. I don't think there are any charcoal-burners left nowadays, for I've never seen any since I was a nipper. Even the woods are not the same nowadays, for many fine trees were felled between 1914 and 1918, and though you can build something like a Georgian or Elizabethan house you can't build a hundred-years'-old oak.

My love for the woods was a great annoyance to my father – he couldn't understand it. With a great park to play in why should a lad want to mope about in the woods? 'The lad's fair daft,' he said, and forbade me going into the woods any more. The chaplain used to say: 'He will be a great man some day, let him study nature if that's his bent.'

Well, both the chaplain and my dad were wrong as far as I can see, with perhaps a slight balance in favour of dad.

Though I wasn't allowed in the woods so often, I made up for it by stealing out through the pantry window when all the family were asleep. I spent nights in the summer watching for the old badger to put his nose out at the badger holes. It was seldom I got a sight of him, but once or twice in the grey light of morning I saw him nose his way among the anemones. I watched the vixen fox play with her cubs by the lake side, and the sparrow-hawk searching the ivy round the houses, and sometimes a white owl would float dangerously near my face, as though it wanted to know what I was doing out.

My parents were Methodists and we were brought up with strict regard for the Sabbath. There was no Nonconformist place of worship nearer than two miles, so we usually went to the private chapel belonging to the House. But sometimes, as a special treat, an anniversary, or thanksgiving, dad and mother would take us to the village chapel. We were always dressed very respectable on Sundays. How mother did it on seventeen shillings a week is one of those mysteries that no mother can solve these days. She was one of the old school, whose life was a constant endeavour to make ends meet – ends that were too wide apart ever to make a straight and lasting joint. Gentle and devoted, she worshipped the virtue of respectability.

Dad and mother walked in front, he carrying a walking-stick and wearing a well-brushed black coat with two large buttons shining in the rear. Mother wore a black bonnet, tied under her chin and all shiny beads nodding about on top. My three sisters and I walked respectfully behind, they with long pigtails hanging down, and I wearing a round pork-pie hat. It was a long two miles, with flowers all the way, which we could not gather on account of its being Sunday. Neither did we black our boots before setting out; that was another sinful action to perform on the Sabbath. It was my duty every Saturday morning, before going out to play, to black six pairs of Sunday boots and put them away in the bottom cupboard. There was no skipping them, either; if they weren't shiny enough they had to be cleaned over again.

Our school was about a mile away, and our schoolmistress the dearest old lady that ever kept school. There were about sixty scholars when all were present, and I thought she must be very wealthy when on occasions she would send each row in turn to the little sweet shop. By the time the last row had been the shop had sold out its stock of sweet-stuff.

An interesting event was when the hounds met at the Hall. Then the children would be taken to see the meet. Whether it went down as a lesson in natural history, or what it was, I don't know, but it was an interesting lesson, watching the pink coats arrive on their prancing horses, and the dappled hounds trotting round the whipper-in. Sometimes the bigger boys would ask leave to follow, and, though leave was granted on condition they got back to school by dinner-time, it was seldom they saw any more school that day. I can't say I have ever been much credit to my good schoolmistress's teaching; reading, writing and drawing were the only subjects I was any good at. I was always a duffer at sums; neither then nor now can I make anything of pounds, shillings and pence, which probably accounts for my still being a farm labourer.

Her chief care for our welfare was to teach us morals and manners, most of which I forgot in the surroundings of my after years. One thing I shall always be grateful for is that she taught me to love and reverence good literature. Although I have never made much success of life – which was no fault of her teaching – life has been made rich because when ploughing up a nest of field-mice I could recite Robert Burns's 'Ode to a Field-mouse'. I have always been fond of poetry, and could recite off-hand much of Burns, Keats, Shelley's 'Skylark' and many of the great poets. I know that farm lads are not credited with much wisdom, but perhaps the general opinion is wrong, for who knows what a farm lad is turning over in his mind as he walks along his furrow? The chaplain, too, encouraged my love of reading, and lent me several boys' books from his library. Thus, at an early age I learned of a world beyond the boundary-wall of the park, and in fancy I journeyed in Lady Brassey's *Sunbeam* or got wrecked on *The Coral Island* or shared *The Adventures of Robinson Crusoe*.

Being fond of reading and drawing, and the study of nature, it was the opinion of my elders and betters that I ought to be put to something. Dad felt very strongly about it, and, being a man of some intelligence and foresight, decided to lift me out of the rut of a farm labourer. It was agreed that, on leaving school, I should be bound apprentice to his brother-in-law, who had a fairly big joinery business in town. But circumstances arose that made of me a farm labourer, and I never regret being one.

Our way of living in the park would seem rather dull nowadays, when buses can pick you up at the park gates and drop you into civilization in a very short time. But I don't think the tenants are any happier, or more contented, for the change. There is not now that personal contact between the big landowners and the tenantry. Taxation and death-duties have reduced the friendly gatherings in the gay ballroom at the House to cheap 'socials'.

Our Christmas treat used to be a splendid affair; the ballroom lit up with tall candles in a row of marvellous-looking chandeliers down the centre of the room. A tall fir tree, weighed down with presents and gay bunting, stood at one end of the room, and round it the youngsters romped and laughed. When the other candles were lighted, the tree became a blaze of coloured lights.

It was the same the night of the workmen's ball, when the Christmas tree was loaded with useful presents, such as clothes and bedding, and the lords and ladies danced with the work-people, and neither side knew the meaning of class distinction.

On the Saturday before Christmas I used to go with mother to help carry home the Christmas beef. A fat beast was cut up in the coach-house down by the stables, and each workman and his wife were given two pounds of beef each, and every child was given one pound. In addition, loaves of bread were given out, and a merry Christmas it made in a large family. The stable-yard was a quiet sort of place as a rule, sacred to the hunters and their grooms. But on this day a lad might peep down the long line of stables without fear of the fat rosy-faced coachman ordering him off. The stable-yard was a big square place with stables and offices all round it. Over the stables were the 'bothies' – the coachman's and grooms' quarters. To reach these you climbed a winding stone stairway and went along side corridors where your boots echoed like a regiment of foot. The whole place seemed to me capable of housing a regiment of cavalry, horse and man. In my childish fancy I likened it to the courtyard at Torquilstone in *Ivanhoe*, with knights in armour clattering over the stone setts. Over all was the pleasant smell of dead horse-chestnut leaves and stable litter. I can smell it now as I write about it.

In one building was housed the fire-engine, an up-to-date affair that went by steam. It was considered a vast improvement on the one we had on the farm buildings, which was a long box-like affair on four wheels. When a haystack caught fire four men stood on each side of this engine and pumped for all they were worth on a long handle running on either side. This, in its turn, had been considered a vast improvement on the chain-bucket system.

While on about Christmas, I ought to mention Christmas Eve at the farm bailiff's. We were all invited into the farm kitchen on Christmas Eve to watch the mummers and the Derby tup. The mummers daubed their faces with lamp-black, red raddle, or chalk. They were dressed up to represent nothing on earth, which isn't to say they looked heavenly. The more face-powder they had used the more inclined were they to kiss the maids under the mistletoe. Then the Derby tup came in, one of the lads crouching under a sheep's skin carrying an ugly staring sheep's head. They then sang a long rigmarole about this wonderful tup, beginning:

As I was going to Derby
All on a market day
Let the finest tup, sir,
That ever was fed on hay.

It went on for about a dozen verses, but the singers, suffering from much refreshment taken at many calls, would get mixed up with the verses, so that the bailiff had to send for the jug to prevent them singing all night. After the tup had disappeared with his grisly head the grown-ups sat round the fire drinking and singing to the melodeon. The women sipped cowslip wine in a sort of genteel way, but the men gulped down strong ale as though they meant it. We children joined in the songs, played snapdragon and bob-apple, until the party broke up at about ten o'clock with many exclamations on the lateness of the hour.

Sometimes, during the winter, life would be brightened by a magic-lantern night. This was a great do and was held in the miller's corn-chamber, as our tiny schoolroom was not large enough for a crowd. This was a long chamber, hung with dusty cobwebs, and to reach it you climbed twelve worn stone steps. I know there were twelve because one counted them, either aloud or mentally, when descending into the darkness. Then, after, crossing the rickety footbridge over the beck, it was pretty good going all the way home.

But the corn-chamber! It was dusty and cobwebby, with a thick beams holding up the roof. Over the beam were piles of empty corn sacks, and sacks had been put along the wall sides to make forms and chairs. The 'better offs' sat in the chairs; the children and parents sat on hard, backless forms, while the big youths sat on comfortable bulging sacks of corn. You couldn't have got those respectable mothers to sit on the corn sacks for any money. There they sat on the hard seats, prim and proper, till their 'hippens' ached, while their big sons reclined in comfort along the wall side. The place was lit by stable lanterns, and, after prayers and the singing of 'From Greenland's Icy Mountains' these were put out and the show began. It was in aid of the Universities Mission to Central Africa, and as there's no set measure to enjoyment, let them scoff who will. We got as much enjoyment out of the miller's granary as you get today watching the latest film at the Tivoli. I used to think it fine fun crossing the park at night-time. You see, a grass path isn't much of a guide in the dark, so we just went east, west, north and south, whichever direction we wanted to be, and kept going until we arrived.

The worst of this out o' way place was when you had run out of anything and had to walk two miles to the village shop. It wasn't often done, because most people knew what they wanted when the grocery man called, which was once a fortnight. But once or twice, with my eldest sister for company, we trudged through the dark to the village. It wasn't the turnpike we minded, but we did feel a bit creepy along the carriage drive where the clipped yews stood out like bogies in the dark, or an owl hooted suddenly just overhead, or perhaps a rabbit would squeal among the bushes where a stoat or some bird of prey had lighted on him. It was all a bit creepy-like for two children, and we were glad enough to get through the lodge gates, where the night was not so black as under the shade of the trees.

The village was only small but to us it seemed a mighty big place, and came next only to London in the matter of population. One of its shops – it boasted of two – was kept by a wrinkled-faced old lady who wore a large print bonnet with the strings hanging loosely down, like Red Riding Hood's grandmother. I was always taken by the way she used to taste at anything to make sure what it was. Evidently she couldn't read labels. I stared with wonder one night. My youngest sister had got a severe cold and we asked for sweet nitre. The old lady took a sip from a row of big glass bottles until she worked her way down to the one marked 'spirits of nitre'. 'This is it,' was all she said, after taking a gulp. She neither gasped, choked, nor made a wry face.

Well, that was the shape of my life until I was eleven: secluded and highly respectable, and the same sort of life was known to every cottage on the estate. Every cottage had the stamp of respectability about it. A church calendar and a case of stuffed animals or birds were to be found in every household. I knew every house by its glass case better than I knew the owner's name. There was the cottage with the fox over the dresser, the one with a brown owl over the chimney-piece; another with an otter carrying a trout; the keeper's lodge with a pheasant.

In fact, everyone seemed to have a stuffed specimen of some kind, and my soul revolted at the sight of them. I might have grown up a prig or a Puritan if my father hadn't been taken bad with diabetes. Before I was twelve years old he died, and with his passing went my chances of being 'put to something'. I was glad to take the first job that turned up, to help mother in her struggle to keep the pot boiling.

Two

SHORT COMMONS

I WAS SORRY TO LEAVE the park and the woods, and my friend the little old mole-catcher, but we had to get out of our cottage to make room for another cowman. Everyone was very kind and sympathetic, for dad had been well liked by everyone, and the chaplain – a large-hearted chap he was – offered us every help until we got settled down again. As I mentioned before, mother was of that old school, independent of outside help in the form of charity, and it was almost an insult to her to offer monetary assistance. I received many kind words of advice from my good friends, the chaplain and the school ma'am, both of whom promised me a great future, if I strove to do right, looked after mother, and trusted in God. I have striven hard on all three points without achieving any greatness, except that I have learned to take things as they come and let the lave go by.

Mother was given a cottage in one of the villages belonging to the estate. It was rent free, except the slight acknowledgment of two shillings and sixpence per year, but even with that it amazes me how she fed and clothed us and still maintained that respectability which was the creed of all estate workers. She was given two days' work a week in the still-room at the House, walking more than two miles each way morning and night. That, and a small substantial supper she was allowed to bring home, kept us going during the first year.

The village at that time had about three hundred inhabitants, and I remember thinking, as we rode in on the top of our dray-load of furniture, what a mighty fine place it was. Mother was given a comfortable seat on the dray front, for it was a raw January day when we moved in, and I thought if only dad had been there too I could make myself quite happy in such a busy village. I counted one grey old church, one Wesleyan Chapel, two inns, two butchers, three grocers and four farms. It was the most populous place I had ever been in, and I longed to start exploring right away.

We had a nice little cottage with roses growing up the walls, and a big garden with half a dozen apple trees in it, and I soon settled down to my new surroundings. I soon found that the village was not so big and important as I had imagined, and my life differed very little from that in the park. I was at this time full of book heroes, determined to do wonderful things in the near future, and to relieve mother from ever having to go out to work again. But I had a lot to learn. For one thing, a fatherless lad has not the liberty the glory-book orphan has – to strap his bundle on his shoulder and seek his fortune. I was tied to home, in a village where agriculture was the only pursuit, with more lads on offer than there were jobs to be had. My uncle sometimes drove over to see how we were managing, and though he would pat me on the head, and in his brisk way advise me to 'look sharp an' grow up so ye can look after yer mam', he was careful not to mention an apprenticeship. Of course, 'being put to something' was now out of the question, as an apprentice worked his three years or more without wage, and a wage was badly needed at our house. But we jogged along very nicely, and we children scarcely felt the loss of that seventeen shillings a week, though we sorely missed the one who had earned it. We had always been taught to 'eat our orts up', and though now at times we didn't know where the next meal was coming from, it somehow came, through mother's wonderful management.

I was now twelve years old, with still another year to put in at school. Folk said 'it wer' a shame a gurt lad like he bein' kep' at school', and 'it wer' a scandless shame as a lad couldn't leave school afore he wer' thirteen to help his mither'. But to school I had to go, though I grumbled at being held back from helping to keep the house. I could have stayed away occasionally, for the education authorities were not so strict in those days, but mother insisted on my getting all the learning I could.

I ought to have made a great success of life by the grand schemes we planned. At night-time, while waiting for mother to come home, my sisters and I would sit round the fire, drawing up wonderful plans for raising more money. Amongst other schemes was one for selling the surplus produce from our garden; but, alas, there wasn't any surplus. When the spring came I took the spade and dug; then I found that even garden seed was not to be had without money. It was disappointing, for I had rare visions of what I could do in the market-garden business. However, I had made some pals at school, and they set me up with their dads' surplus garden seed. When summer came I had as good a show of weeds and plants as anyone in the village. The village in those days was a popular resort for visitors, and my eldest sister – she was thirteen and always more practical than ever I was – got the idea of selling flowers. It was a come-down for a lad of twelve, but I have never since felt anything like the joy of having a fist full of money as when one Saturday afternoon we spied eighteen pennies on the table, our first result of selling flowers. We did well at it, and when the garden failed we searched the woods and fields, and were surprised to find so many willing to give a penny for a bunch of wild flowers.

My sister left school soon after she was thirteen, and minded the house while mother was out at work. Being practical, and with always an eye to business, she started making teas, and did quite well at it until she went into domestic service. Quite a lot of cottages in the village had 'Tea or Hot Water' posted in the windows. We had jolly times, too, and when our tea-drinkers had gone we indulged in amusing speculations as to who they were, their names, and what they did for a living. They would have felt flattered had they heard us, for we generally concluded that they were lord and lady somebody, or even duchesses and princesses, instead of which they probably were ordinary people like ourselves, just out for the day.

I was never any good at business myself, and my only effort in that direction broke my bank. A lad could often earn a copper or two by holding horses outside the Black Swan. There would be a long line of wagonettes, traps, buggies and all manner of horse-drawn vehicles wanting their horses minded while the parties went inside for a drink. A number of my schoolmates gathered coppers in this way on Saturday afternoons and holiday times but I had been expressly forbidden from holding horses outside pubs. Mother, as I said before, was a Methodist, and to her mind I should become defiled if I held a horse outside a pub. But I had to do it. Not daring to let mother know, I spent the money I had earned in buying a couple of tame rabbits off another lad; I told her that I had them given to me, and she asked no further questions. I looked forward to making a living out of rabbits; the lad I bought them off did very well in that line of business, so why not I?

I made a run for them on the grass in the day time, keeping them in the hutch at night. I knew that in the matter of rearing animals I could beat my pal, but unfortunately my outside run was a very flimsy affair of empty boxes. I came home from school one dinner-time to find them lying dead on the garden path and a white terrier dog nosing about in the run. I have to confess I cried with vexation and temper, and, worse than that, I blamed my sister for letting the dog get into the garden. Then she cried, and the two youngest coming in for dinner, seeing that tears were in favour, joined in too.

The only advantage I got out of rabbits was that they saved our dinner for that day, for none of us could eat, on account of our disaster. When mother came home she advised me to see the dog-owner about it, cautioning me to remember my manners. The owner of the dog was a retired business man, very highly respected throughout the village. His name headed the list of subscribers for most of the charitable causes in the place, so I expected no difficulty in laying my case before him. I waited outside his gates some time, watching for him coming out. I never had much pluck, and felt shy of knocking at his door; besides which, I knew he always went down to the 'Swan' about eight o'clock every night. So I waited and watched. When he came out I approached him timidly, and said: 'Please, sir – '

I got no further, for he had seen me hanging about and drove me off with his stick. Evidently I was not a charitable object, or the fault may be I was too backward at coming forward, so I gave up rabbit–keeping as a bad job.

I did manage to earn quite a lot of money that summer, and it came about in this way. School holidays were arranged to suit the farmers; at least, Whitsuntide and harvest holidays. If Whitsun came early we had one week then and five weeks in harvest. If Whitsun fell when the turnips were ready for singling we got two or three weeks' holiday according to the convenience of the farmers, with either three or four weeks for harvest. No matter which way it came, most of the lads, and lassies, too, spent their holidays singling turnips. And what a back-aching job it was! But I enjoyed it after the first few days. Along with two other lads I worked a fortnight at a shilling a day during the Whitsun holiday, and listened, I have to confess, with relish, to the coarse jokes of the men hoeing turnips. I did even better in the summer, putting five weeks at turnip singling without missing a day, staying a week longer than the school holiday.

We had got to know a man who came to chapel, a steady, God-fearing man, who, though only a farm worker, was a local preacher, and he, knowing our needs, offered me work enough to last all summer. He was on piecework, getting so much an acre for striking-out, and he paid me one and sixpence a day to single after him. That was good pay, as most lads got a shilling a day for singling turnips. But, oh dear, I shall never forget that five weeks – it was the longest holiday I have ever had. I worked from six a.m. to six p.m. and six days a week. But I stuck it, and proudly took home nine shillings each Saturday night. The painful part about it was his being on piecework, for then the striker leaves more plants for his singler to pull out, and I bent over the hot earth till the blood ran into my head and I couldn't see whether I'd left two plants or one.

Day after day I stooped along the rows with the scorching sun blistering my neck, and no one to talk to but old Amos, and I often thought wistfully of my summers in the cool wood, and of the spotted does hiding in the bracken. Had there been two lads singling instead of my being alone, the days would not have seemed so long; but five weeks with Amos at twelve hours a day would turn a saint. Scarcely a word was spoken all day, except for a few sentences as we sat under the hedge in the dinner-hour. I hope I am a Christian, but I can't help thinking now, as I thought then, that saints do very well for Sundays, but for everyday wear you can't beat a good owd sinner. But I ought to say a word in favour of old Amos, for he was a staunch old-time Methody, and would tramp miles on Sundays to preach at some chapel or other in the circuit, and this in spite of the fact he walked with a stoop, giving the impression of having tender feet. For this reason we children called him Mister Tenderfoot, taking care not to let mother hear us. He had a zeal for Methodism not to be found in this generation. He was a regular plodder, and though he had enough cares of his own, found time to help us with our garden. Had he not been so silent during my five weeks' holiday I might have called him lovable.

I have always had a liking for the Methodists, and though during my years in farm service I managed very well without creeds of any sort, I always found pleasure in whistling a good old Moody and Sankey when ploughing. We had been strictly brought up while dad was alive, and now mother, though often too tired to correct every little fault, kept us under a firm hand. We attended the church Sunday school morning and afternoon – there being no Sabbath school at the chapel – and mother took us to chapel for evening service. Even during my five weeks' turnip singling, when to lie in bed on Sunday morning would hardly be called a serious fault, I had to be out and at school for nine-thirty. Mother allowed no malingering.

The chapel was a quaint little place, and what I remember most about it was the choir. Though small in numbers it had the reputation of having the best tenor singer in the village. To hear 'Thias Applewick was to hear a bit of singing to remember. 'Thias was the village wheelwright, and a great singer. He was a stout man, with a yellow moustache, the corners of which hung down like a pair of tusks. When Miss Lovebond began to play, 'Thias would get on his feet in readiness. Then, when the hymn began, he would stand with his chest thrust forward and his head thrown back so that I always expected to see him topple over. He never did topple over, but led the little choir with gusto, holding his book at arm's length, and glancing first at his book and then at the old harmonium – or perhaps at

Miss Lovebond, but I think it was the harmonium.

There were five people in the choir, including 'Thias, and the congregation seldom numbered more than a dozen. After the service came a prayer meeting, so called, but mostly it was a service of song. After a short prayer by the preacher, John Loundes would say: 'Nah, Mr Applewick, let's have the owd favourite, "Oh land of rest for thee I sigh",' and 'Thias would lead off, still keeping one eye on the old harmonium. When that was finished someone would start another, for they did enjoy a bit of singing, that handful of people, and I can't see myself as there's any better way of showing thankfulness than by singing.

The village was sharply divided between church and chapel, though there was a strong element who favoured the Black Swan or the Jug and Glass to either. But the 'churchers' looked down on the 'chapellers', while the 'chapellers' thought the 'churchers' a stuck-up lot. Be that as it may, they wouldn't mix, and even the vicar failed to recognise anyone who went to chapel. But the most bitter person against the chapel was the sexton; 'they ranters', he used to call them. He was the most important person in the village, and even the vicar seemed almost afraid of Johnny Clark. You might ignore the vicar, or the doctor, but no one dared ignore the sexton, for he had a finger in everyone's pie. Officiating at the three most important events in their lives had given him inside information about every person in the village, and he was the greatest authority on who's who to the length of four generations. He was also godfather to nearly every child in the village, and, except for giving them presents, I believe he fulfilled his office with credit. From his short pew near the font he kept his eye on us during children's service, and no matter how we dared defy the reproving looks of the school teacher, so soon as Johnny Clark's boots gave a creak we all sat straight and proper.

He had a great aversion to 'these 'ere ranters', the chapel-goers, and to 'Thias Applewick in particular. 'Thias being the sole undertaker for the village, he and the sexton were, in a way, bound together in business, and for that reason the sexton thought that 'Thias should be a member of the Church of England. The story used to be told how, one hot summer, the vicar held prayers for rain, and still the drought continued, so he decided to call on the Nonconformist party for united effort. Johnny Clark was sadly put out about calling in the 'ranters', and prophesied 'no good would come of it'. It happened, that same night of united prayer, a terrific thunderstorm broke over the district, washing Farmer Merril's turnips out of the hill field into the beck and doing lots of damage. Johnny saw the wreckage next morning, and said: 'It's them ranters! I knew how it 'ud be, fetchin' them ranters in, they allus overdo it.'

As I attended both church and chapel regularly, and as one of my failings in life has been along the lines of W.H. Davies's poem – 'to stand and stare', I distinctly remember the different atmosphere between church and chapel. The congregation at church was mostly of 'the quality', while the chapel took in the tradespeople, excepting Mr Ounceby, who kept the largest of the grocers' shops. He attended church dressed in a frock-coat and a tall silk hat, and always wore a flower in-his buttonhole.

To be quite fair, I must admit, the only people to take an interest in the sick and needy were certain devout ladies who attended church every Sunday. The chapel folk might shake hands all round; but it was not a giving hand.

In church, the most noticeable thing, if you sat near the middle aisle, was the long row of chimney-pot hats placed at the pew ends. I think it was the chimney-pots that gave to the church that cold stern atmosphere, for most of the people were pleasant, and the vicar was a most worthy Christian gentleman.

And now about the people who preferred the Black Swan or the Jug and Glass. Most writers about country-folk unearth some quaint, amusing characters, but our village had no outstanding personalities; just plain hard-working country-folk. Being Yorkshire people they had the true Yorkshireman's love of horse flesh, and in the days before the motor it was the desire of everyone who had saved a pound or two to own a horse. It didn't matter whether they'd any work for a horse or not, the great idea was to 'knock about wi' a hoss'.

I remember Sam Tracey won ten pounds that September on the St Leger

– on Rock Sand I believe it was – and he bought a 'hoss' with his winnings. It wasn't much of an animal at ten pounds, but I believe every man in the village handled it and gave his opinion on it during its first week at Sam's. It had broken knees, a wall eye, and a spavin on its off-side hock, according to different authorities. When Farmer Moore asked: 'What made thi buy a thing like that?' Sam replied: 'I bought him to ate a bit o' gress.'

In truth there seemed no other reason, unless it was the Yorkshireman's love for a bit o' horse flesh. Having no work to put it to, he lent it out to a coal dealer – work for keep – but as it turned out a jibber it was eventually turned out on the common, and when winter came it 'got down' and was sold to the knacker man for fifty shillings.

The common was a large piece of waste land, amounting to some twenty acres or thereabouts. In summer it was grazed by ponies, nags and galloways of all kinds, while very often it was the camping ground for gypsies. How so many horses made a living on such short commons was no doubt best known to themselves, for most of it was covered with bracken and short, stunted silver birch trees. It made a rare playground for the village youngsters, however, and I never saw a better spot for linnets and goldfinches. The pig population being almost as large as the human one – nearly every cottager kept a pig – the bracken was mown and carried home for bedding, and I thought it rare fun helping the more fortunate lads, who had a pig in the family, to gather bracken, whether by wheelbarrow or cart.

An event of some importance in the village, especially to the lads, was pig-killing morning. As there would be a matter of twenty or more pigs to be killed during the winter, and as every cottager liked his pig-killing on Saturday morning, so that it could hang over the weekend before being cut and salted, and as everyone wanted their pig-killing 'with a rising moon' so that the flitches would take salt properly, well, it made pig-killing morning an exciting time. All the neighbours had pig's fry for dinner on that day, and a number of children could be seen trotting backwards and forwards carrying pig's fry trapped between two plates. There was one condition to be observed about these plates. They must be returned unwashed, else it would wash away the luck from the pig. Not that the pig was in any way concerned about luck, it wasn't his lucky day anyhow, but it was a custom to be observed at all costs, and once when a young girl washed the plates, she not knowing any different, there was no end of a to-do. The neighbours gathered round the pig-owners' cottage and sympathised with them, as though the pig had disappeared there and then. Whether it proved unlucky or not I never heard, but I remember on Sunday morning several children at the Sunday school telling each other how so-and-so had washed a fry plate, which shows how serious an event it was.

Once or twice during the winter I stayed away from school to go bush-beating. This was real fun, and besides getting one and sixpence for the day and a couple of rabbits, I was back in my favourite woods. The head keeper had been a near neighbour and a personal friend of dad's, so he went out of his way to let me be one of his beaters when a shooting-party was arranged. There would be the usual big house-party of earls, dukes, and county families out for a day with the birds, while keepers, gardeners and estate workmen were called up to drive the woods and beat the bushes. It was playing Indians to some purpose, with a long line of beaters stretched across the wood. We pushed our way among hazels, scrambled through brambles, driving the game towards the guns. The guns walked along the ridings and the edge of the wood.

About one o'clock we came to one of the main ridings, where a big copper on wheels awaited us. It was the gentry's lunch hour and the beaters' dinner-time. We all sat down under a wide-spreading yew, and kicked off with soup. Not clear soup by any means, for you took a plate to the man at the copper, and there saw carrots, rabbit legs and bits of ragged meat bobbing up and down as though trying to jump out of the boiling cauldron. Then came rabbit or chicken pie with bread and cheese to follow, along with a can of ale. For those who didn't take ale there was coffee to be had off the game wagon, and altogether it was a delightful feast out there in the autumn or winter woods. It was a delight, too, to be eating with the tall, silent trees standing around, and the brown leaves lying all curled up on the squelchy cart-track, and the occasional drip-drip of melting dew on the fringes of the yew tree.

Although I enjoyed the scramble through the woods, it was a bit sickening to see the handsome cock pheasants, their lovely wings bent backwards, come crashing through the trees, to fall with a thump on the soft earth. It wasn't fair, nor sporting, to slaughter them off like so. Partridges and rabbits were different, they were completely wild, but the pheasants were fed and reared by the hundreds in coops and pens. They were half-tame, so that there was little sport in shooting at them. Well, as I always brought home a couple of rabbits and enjoyed eating the same, I've no need to grieve over his lordship's pheasants. Anyhow I wouldn't like to eat one after the fashion of the gentry. I have afore times watched the housekeeper inspecting the game larder. She would walk along the rows of hanging pheasants, clasping her hands, looking very stately and prim, and exclaiming: 'Beautifully high! beautifully high!' while great fat maggots fell to the ground. Bah! Well, times have changed, and there are not so many pheasants reared nowadays, on account of the coalfield; and from the same cause, our village, which was then a beauty spot of three hundred souls, is now a flourishing mining town of twelve thousand inhabitants.

Our fortunes began to mend after our first year, and mother went to work less often, doing fairly well at making teas for summer visitors. As we became better known to the gentry of the village, so we fared the better. Mother, being a good needlewoman, soon found plenty of work from the big houses – there being more hand-stitching done then than now – and so we thrived, and might have enlarged the floor of our tent, but for those old country creeds. Like so many of the old school, mother had two pet rules which governed her life. One was: 'Thou shalt not run into debt'; and the other: 'Thou shalt not show thy poverty before strangers.' They drove her hard, and, while many of the children in the village were ragged and unkempt, to her honour we were always kept clean and respectable. For which reason many of the neighbours said: 'Sho's a bit of a pension comin' in, else sho couldna' do it.' But she did do it. And she had no pension.

Three

THE DAY-LAD

IN MARCH 1904, being three months turned of my thirteenth birthday, I was able to leave school. I got work on a farm as day-lad at one and threepence a day, working from six-thirty a.m. to five-thirty p.m., and very proud I was to get a regular job so easily, and proud I was to carry home on Saturday night three bright half-crowns.

The farm was on top of a steep hill, about a mile outside the village, and was kept by a widow woman with a rather shrewish tongue. A tall, raw-boned woman she was, with skirts permanently tucked up aft, and wearing a black hat of no particular shape. She was as hefty as a young navvy, and as strong as a young horse. She tackled any kind of work that turned up, such as slicing turnips for the beasts, teaming loads of hay, or even assisting at calving a cow. She was never lost for a job, but was always on the go, for which reason I probably got the job so easily.

It was a four-horse place. We never called a farm as having so many acres. That is, we reckoned a pair of horses for each fifty acres of plough-land, with an extra horse for odd jobs and busy times. So as near as I can say, we had about a hundred acres of plough and thirty acres of grassland. This method of reckoning wouldn't do nowadays, when so much arable land has been seeded down and the tractor has displaced the horse for ploughing.

It was a four-horse place with two horse chaps and a cowman, when I became engaged as a day-lad. My first job was scaring crows off the barley, a job I greatly enjoyed at first, but soon found rather monotonous and lonesome. I had three fields to scare all in a line with each other, and, as the birds were just beginning to nest in the hedgerows, I was able to scare crows and do a bit of birds' nesting at the same time. But the weather came on colder, and one day it began to rain; a cold, driving sleet that drove me into the plantation running alongside the far field. I stayed in the wood seeking birds' nests long after the rain had stopped, and when I came out I found the crows very busy on the barley. I shouted 'shoo' to scare them away, and that gave George an idea of my whereabouts.

George was the bailiff-wagoner, and had been looking for me to give him a hand with the ewes and lambs. So, after a kick in my rear, he took me away from crow-tending and set me on to tend sheep, cautioning me with what would happen if he caught me in the wood again. I found tending the sheep much more pleasant than tending crows, though much busier. The hedges were in a bad state of repair, and I was supposed to keep the sheep from straying, but there were so many gaps that to keep them in was impossible. Two 'massams' in particular I was always having to chase out of the barley or the turnips. There were twenty-six ewes with thirty-four lambs, and every night I had to drive them home into the croft, counting them through the gate to make sure none were missing.

One Saturday night I counted them through, but couldn't make more than twenty-four of the ewes – the massams were missing. Being Saturday night I said nothing, hoping I had miscounted them, and trusted in Providence to make them right for Monday morning. But Providence doesn't make wrong right, and when I got to the farm on Monday morning there was the missus waiting by the croft gate. I didn't like the look of her eye when she asked: 'Nah, my lad, an ye counted these shipe o' late?'

I answered: 'Yes, I counted 'em on Sat'day.'

'Oh, ye did, did yer? Well, ma lad, we'll count 'em agin this morning to mak' sure.'

So I ran round my little flock while she stood in the gateway 'telling' them through one by one.

'Twenty-four. Mebbe we counted wrong; fetch 'em back,' she said.

So I fetched them back again, and she counted them several times like that, having me running back and forth until I had to admit there were only twenty-four. She then lifted me up by the scruff of the neck and shook me well – she being a hefty sort of woman, there was no chance of wriggling free – and told the two 'massams' had been in Bennett's barley since Saturday.

I passed several weeks minding the ewes and lambs in the new clover, and the days passed pleasantly enough. Then Harry, the cowman, came with a load of stakes and fencing material and I had to help him, though I looked on more than helped, to mend the gaps in the hedge. After that there was no further need to mind sheep, so I went along with Harry, weeding corn and, later on, hoeing turnips.

Another job I had was seeking hen eggs for the missus. This was a spare-time job, for which I got one penny per score, and hoped thereby to raise some pocket money. Alas, for my hopes I seldom raised more than a penny a week. Neither then nor now have I been much of a hand at melding money. The great drawback to this scheme was the missus. She went round first, collecting from the hen roost, the cart-shed, and other easily accessible places, while I was left to the hen that laid astray. However, I bought a penny notebook to tot up my egg money as I sat having my dinner in the stable. Not having much totting up to do, I found another use for my note book. Being fond of writing and drawing, I filled it with sketches of animals and people on the farm, some of them having a slight resemblance to the missus. Also I turned it into a diary. This is a habit I have kept up by fits and starts ever since. One day it fell out of my pocket and George picked it up. I expected some 'boot-toe' when he had finished looking through it, 'boot-toe' being the recognised form of correction for farm lads. He called to the missus to come and see, and there we stood by the fold-yard gate, I waiting for the kick that was sure to come when they had done looking at my sketches. But the kick didn't come that time, and evidently the missus didn't recognise her own likeness, for all she said was: 'Hoos a gradely speller, but I doot if hoo 'l ever mak' a farmer.'

When haytime came I was set to drive carts and to 'loaden' hay. I found

loading hay a difficult task until I got the 'how' of it. I would be stood atop
of the load, to feel it slowly slipping from under my feet, and, with the
next jolt of the cart, over would go the hay with me buried underneath.
If George was in the field, I got more boot as an aid to learning the art of
loading hay, but usually he was in the stack-yard, so the other helpers just
laughed at my efforts, and we started all over again. It was thirsty work,
too, and as ale was the only drink offered to haymakers, and as I had been
brought up to avoid any kind of strong drink, I suffered greatly from thirst.
But not for long, however. I thought of all the cowslips I had gathered for
mother 'agen Christmas coming', and all the jolly do's I had seen where
men made merry over a glass of good ale, and saw no harm in a lad taking
a sip in the hayfield. So in the end I slaked my thirst at the stone bottle and
learned the art of loading hay.

I had better have remained thirsty, for the men called me a hero and
kidded me on to drink again. With the bravado of a lad of thirteen I drank
again, though I didn't like the taste of it. And saying: 'We'll mak' a man
of ye yet', they plied me with strong ale until the haycocks began to swim
and I was terribly sick in the hedge bottom. It was only fun on their part,
but George came into the field as I was heaving my heart up, and set me
off home with his boot-toe, where I got a severe wigging for breaking the
pledge. After that the missus found me a can of tea every afternoon when
we worked late, which was until about eight-thirty, the men getting their
usual ale for afternoon drinkings.

It was a jolly life – having tea in the field, sitting under a haycock, and
I thought farm work the finest game on earth. I was always hungry, and I
don't suppose, even in those cheap-living days, there was much change left
over of my seven shillings and sixpence after I had been fed. My clothes
didn't cost much in the summer, for the simple reason I didn't wear many.
A white linen hat, shirt, trousers down to my knees, stockings, and a pair
of worn-out boots were all I needed until colder days came. I felt a bit
conceited when, after the hay was gathered, I went hoeing turnips in the
field where some school lads were singling during their summer holidays.
It's surprising how one year's progress lifts you over your neighbours – or

at least you think so.

At harvest-time I was shown how to make bands, while we opened out the ten-acre oats. Arthur, our seconder, mowed a swathe round the field, while Harry 'took up'. Arthur was a youth of nineteen but I looked upon him as a grown man, he seemed such a long way ahead of me. My work was to make bands and tie up. It was a busy job, and I was glad not to be making them for George. I never put the bands in the right place for Harry to swing his sheaf across, but I found, as I grew older, no one ever does. He would swear occasionally at having to wait while I twisted another band or boxed up a sheaf, but he was a decent sort and kept his boot in the stubble.

After the field was opened out I rode the first horse for George in the binder; that is, George drove Flower and Violet at the pole, whilst I rode old Short in sling-chains in front. It was a nice, easy job, though it got uncomfortable to the trouser seat when old Short began to sweat, and, the two pole horses being young and fresh, I was constantly being shouted at to 'touch the old horse up a bit'. However, I had a happy time of it; riding first horse until we had got all our corn cut.

Then, one day, two Irishmen turned up, and George set them on stooking the sheaves. Quite a lot of Irishmen used to come round in those days to do a bit of harvesting, and these two came regularly to Hill-top for the harvest. Sometimes they stayed on to help with the potatoes, and while they were there they lodged in the chop-chamber. They set the corn up (stooked) at so much an acre, with ale found, and when leading, picked and loaded the carts by the acre too. They found their own victuals, excepting 'ale 'lowance', and always had a 'nine galloner' in the chop place, which stunk pretty strongly of sour ale and foul clothes when they went away.

They stayed that year to help with the potatoes, and I never saw anyone eat so many spuds as did those two Irishmen. They boiled potatoes by the basketful in the yard near the cart-shed, boiling them in the skins, and then stabbing a long-bladed knife amongst the potatoes, peeled off the skins, and gobbled them up as they stood round the bucket. The potatoes smelled good, done in that way, but the Irishmen didn't.

When the sheaves were gathered, I was sent to horse-rake the stubbles with old Short. He was the first horse I had ever driven, and very proud I was of him. He was an old horse, dark brown in colour, with white feet behind and a white mark down his forehead. I was at a disadvantage compared with most village lads in that while I knew a lot about woodcraft and keepers and mole-catchers I knew very little about what comes next on a farm, though I soon picked it up under George's tuition and came to know the meaning of 'there's nothing like leather'. Consequently I made more fuss over old Short than most lads would do, though all lads were horse-proud in those days. During my dinner-hour, while George and the 'seconder' were in the house, I would run with a measure of meal for my horse. This went on for several days until the old horse got 'stalled' with so much corn, and George found his manger full of dry meal and old Short off his feed. I got more 'boot-toe' for meddling, and thereby learned how to feed horses.

After the rakings were picked up I helped Harry, the cowman, to thatch the stacks; at least, I handed up the bats and pegs while he did the thatching. It was interesting work, too, and I was taken up by the neat way he fitted one row of bats over the other, and would soon have learned how it was done had not the orchard been so near. About the middle of the forenoon Harry would say: 'Is shoo hanging about?' meaning, of course, the missus.

I would look round and say: 'No, I don't see her anywhere.'

Then Harry would say: 'What about a few pears?'

Of course, I got caught at it, and only escaped a wigging by dodging the missus around the corn stacks.

After this I was set on to pull apples and pears. I thought I could manage this job very nicely; but no such luck, for the missus came with me. I stared with amazement, too, at the way she reared a long ladder up against the pear tree and nipped up it with a basket in one hand and a hooked stick in the other. There was too much of her. She could get about like a two-year-old, and I had always thought I could scrim up a tree with the next, but she beat me hollow at reaching for apples and pears. She never let one fall to the ground, a thing I was always doing, especially if I thought she was looking. Then she would call out, 'Butter fingers, ye'll demmock all the apples i' the orchard!' and that would cause me to drop another. But I don't think she was a bad sort really, it was her having such a shrewish tongue, and my being very young and a bit timid of her. By the time we had finished pulling apples I got more used to her and she seemed quite amiable.

After the stacks were thatched down the cowman went brushing hedges, and I was given a pair of horses and taught to plough. Short was my line-horse, with the trap mare, Betsey, in the furrow, and a more ill-assorted pair it would be hard to imagine. Short was a steady-going old plodder, while Betsey the trap mare was eager to be going, and Short's steady pace irritated her till she went wild with excitement. I made slow progress in learning to plough, and not till after many days' treatment between George and the 'seconder' did I learn to draw a straight furrow. I was neither big enough nor strong enough to turn the plough on the headland – I didn't stand much higher than the plough stilts – and the trap mare would keep getting a leg over the chains when turning at the ends. Then round she would spin, kicking and jumping; over would go the plough, with me clinging on and ready to cry with vexation. George and Arthur would laugh at my distress before coming to my assistance. Then, after setting me in order again, would speed the plough with the application of more boot.

There was nothing unusual about their method of teaching; they had been taught the selfsame way, and were only carrying on the old tradition – that the only way to learn is to find out. A lad was never shown how to do a thing; to show him how was to spoil him. The only way to learn either ploughing, thatching, stacking, or any other skilled work, was to watch how other people did it, and then earn your skill by trial and error. Happily that method is not in force today, though it had much to recommend it, for a lad took more notice of how a thing was done by watching someone else than he would by someone showing him just how, while the boot no doubt impressed it on his memory.

So by this gentle method I learned to plough, and soon found ploughing the pleasantest job on the farm; at least, I always liked it the best, and by the way most plough lads sing and whistle you can bet they are enjoying the work. There is artistry in drawing a clean, straight furrow. Simple as it looks, it's not every Tom, Dick and Harry that can do it.

We were 'chipping' stubbles; that is to say, ploughing about three inches deep to turn over the rubbish before fallowing down. The stubbles were then dragged and harrowed until the rubbish lay on the top and was burned. One thing I have always noticed when chipping stubbles, you turn over scores of field mice, nests of them, pink and naked. They are thrown on the ploughing, and you seldom see them at other times, only after harvest. As a lad I always felt like stopping to rescue the little beggars, but a flock of crows following behind soon cleared the furrow of any mouse not big enough to run away.

After the stubbles were cleaned, George and Arthur went ploughing 'clover-ley' for autumn wheat, and I learned another job that was new to me. With old Short I had to press the seams with a 'two-row presser'. Ploughing and pressing for wheat was a highly important piece of work, and after a skilled ploughman like George the pressed seams became a work of art. I felt the importance of my part of the work, too, and was careful to set-in square at the ends, for the wheat was then sown broadcast on the ploughing and came up in neat straight lines nine inches apart. A field sown in this way is worth stopping to look at, and our twelve-acre was the talk of all the farm chaps round about. In those days we used to take a pride in ploughing and sowing, and Sunday morning would see a group of horse chaps examining each other's work, so our twelve-acre was examined by nearly all the chaps in and about the village.

I began to improve a lot under George's tuition, so that he said I was getting 'handy with a pair of 'osses' and ought to think of getting 'hired come Martlemas'. His boot-toe and my seat met less often, and, like a young colt, I soon became 'broken to all gears'.

After the harvest there was threshing to be done. I had always looked on the threshing-machine as rather a grand affair, and I found now that threshing barley was a very ticklish business. It was, and still is, the lad's business to rake away the chaff as it comes pothering out of the riddles, and a dirtier, dustier job is not to be found round the thresher. In my short trousers, not able to sport a pair of leggings, I got stuck with barley ains, and my eyes and throat filled with dust.

After the barley was threshed we delivered it to the malt-kilns in town. Barley was the main crop on most farms when ale was the main drink and cost only twopence-halfpenny per pint, and livering or teaming the barley was a kind of ceremony equal to a May Day procession. The horseman went first with his team, usually three horses in single file, then came the 'seconder' with a pair of horses, while the lad came last with a horse and cart. The first two teams had heavy block drays, or, some of them, big lumbering quarter-lock wagons with double shafts. The chief thing, however, was the decorations. The horses were loaded with 'caddis' plaited in mane and tail. The harness, all cleaned up for the occasion, was bedecked with martingales, face-brasses, bells, hip-straps and as much shining brass as the horse chaps' means would gather together. The only fault with this 'barley livering' was that the wagoners were inclined to come home 'market merry'. It was a point of honour to see how much barley you could carry to town and how much beer you could carry home. When George came home 'market merry' I always kept at a safe distance, for, while he was a quiet sort of chap when sober, after he'd had one or two it always roused his fighting blood, and somehow he seemed to fancy me for his sparring-partner.

In October we started getting up the potatoes and mangolds. The two Irishmen forked up the first lot, while the later potatoes were ploughed out and 'pied' down for winter. A gang of women and girls came to pick them up, and the Irishmen emptied their buckets and baskets into the carts, which I drove to the 'pie', where the cowman covered them over with wheat straw and clamped them down with soil.

I began to fancy myself a bit at this time, thinking I was now grown up, and if any of the girls lagged behind I ordered them to hurry up in as gruff a voice as I could muster. But, alas, it was a poor imitation of George's voice, and while it had very little effect on the girls, it had so much effect on the women that they boxed my ears.

I lacked dignity. I was still dressed like a school kid, with bare knees showing below my trousers, and I felt a bit put out about it. Also I still attended the church Sunday school, and the more I thought of these things, the more convinced was I that I ought to chuck it if I was to win the dignity and respect due to a horseman. So I mentioned the Sunday school to mother, and my dignity was still further lowered when she said: 'You'll keep on with Sunday school till I tell you to stop, and there's an end on't.' Over my short trousers I fared much better. They were about done for anyway, and mother sat up far into the night cutting down a pair of dad's knee-breeches until they were my size, there or thereabouts. They were a bit on the roomy side, but restored my lost dignity; though I am afraid I was not over grateful, considering the amount of overtime they had cost mother.

So I got my hand in at most of the jobs on a farm, and wouldn't now be a joiner for worlds. I thought farming the best job on earth, or under the earth, for that matter, and rode old Short to the field whisthing 'Rosie O'Grady' as merry as a cock blackie at nesting-time.

It was somewhere toward the 'back-end' – we were harrowing the wheat second time over – when George asked me about living in, as Arthur was leaving at Martlemas. Then at noon the missus asked me: 'I dunna want a day-lad; I want a lad to live in an' help wi' the bits o' jobs.'

So we talked it over at home. My eldest sister was now in service, we had a young man lodging with us, and mother was doing fairly well with bits of sewing and making teas. My wage was to be two shillings and sixpence per week with my board and keep in place of my seven shillings and sixpence and live at home. The change seemed all to the good, half a crown a week being a big wage for a lad, the usual rate being a five-pound note for a lad's first year. And so I decided to live in, and became a hired servant.

Four

THE HIRELING

MARTLEMAS WEEK began on 24th November, and all hired servants – men and maids – left their places and had a week's holiday until December, when they either 'stayed on' with the same master or got hired at the Statutes Fair to go to a fresh place. As I had got engaged without going to the 'Stattis', as we called it, I trudged up to Hill-top Farm on 1st December with a green tin box on my shoulder, which pressed hard on my neck before I had done staggering up the steep hill.

It was not my wardrobe that weighed so heavily in my box; my wardrobe consisted of one grey knickerbocker suit for Sundays, two clean shirts and collars, two pairs of stockings, and a pair of Sunday boots. The weight came from a number of books, mostly school prizes, which I fondly imagined I was going to read in my spare time. I reckoned wrong as usual, for I never opened a book until the following Martlemas. I can well remember that first night, leaving my home, the striving and scheming; the skimping a bit here and a bit there that had gone on for weeks so that I might go out into the world clean and respectable, with a complete change of linen. I was not yet fourteen, and I remember that bit of a swagger, which was mostly 'put on', as I said goodbye to mother and sisters before shouldering my box and setting off to seek my fortune. I was still pretty well steeped in 'book heroes' which must be my excuse for thinking that fame and fortune were to be won at Hill-top.

The farm wasn't a bad 'living place'; there being plenty to eat. The trouble was I hadn't enough time to eat in. The missus had said she 'wanted a lad to live in for to do the odd jobs'. She kept no maid, saying she 'wouldna' be pelted wi' sich wenches as ther' is nowadays', and preferred doing all the housework herself. Which was a fallacy, for that was where my odd jobs came in. From morning to night she kept me on the run doing odd jobs, so that during meal times I was running in and out like a dog at a fair.

The kitchen where we had our meals was a big square place, with a stone-flagged floor scrubbed and scoured till it shone cold and bare as charity. A big solid-looking table stood in the centre, and here George and the missus had their meals, my seat being at the side-table near the door, which was handier for the odd jobs. A stone slab with a pump stood near the window overlooking the courtyard. Opposite the window was a place with a shining cooking-range, in front of which was a solitary hearth rug, the only bit of covering that wide expanse of flags. There George, the missus and Laddie the sheepdog warmed their toes; but never the toes of the hired lad. On one side of the fire-place hung a long-handled copper warming-pan, and on the other side stood a bright copper kettle, neither of which was ever used, and, by the way they shone, might never have been used. Two brass candlesticks stood on the chimney-piece and a pair of brass snuffers hung under a cake merchant's almanac in the centre. In one corner stood a grandfather clock with a spray of roses painted across its dial. Several rows of hams and flitches, and a double-barrelled gun, hung from the ceiling, and that was the furnishing of that great kitchen, where everything was scrubbed and scoured and uncomfortable.

We got up at five o'clock every morning, excepting Sunday, when we laid in an hour longer. I cleaned out the stable while George fed and watered the horses. Then I went to the cowshed and milked four cows – dairying was only a sideline in those days, beef and barley being the main products – and took the milk into the house on the stroke of six. Breakfast was at six prompt. If I went in at three minutes past, the missus would say: 'Tha wants ta sharpen thi sen up in a mornin'; 'ere tha's bin an hour a-milkin' four cows, an' corves awaiting for their parridge.'

I learned to have my breakfast with one eye on that calf-porridge. I had fat boiled bacon, with a basin of milk, for breakfast, and had never got very far into it before the missus would jerk the calf-porridge off the fire, saying: "Ere, ma lad, jist nip wi' this afore it gets cow'd. Ye can finish ateing when ye come back.'

We reared about half a dozen calves – the bigger ones having a 'calf meal-porridge' in place of new milk – so I nipped and fed the calves. Sometimes, when I wanted to get back to my breakfast, or I hadn't got a good start beforehand, I spilled some of the porridge in the straw to speed the process, but even that didn't always 'save my bacon' – or perhaps it did – for the missus would meet me in the doorway with the coal-scuttle, saying: "Ere y' are, jist fill this while ye 'r on ye 'r feet!' And in this free-and-easy way I got my breakfast.

It was unfortunate for me that she should be so punctual, for so soon as ever I started eating again George would rise to go, and, as we 'bridled-out' at six-thirty – daylight permitting – the missus would indulge in sarcastic comments on my 'sittin' gorgin' aw' day'. So I learned to 'gollop' my food.

After breakfast I helped the cowman to feed the stock, staggering along under heavy skeps of meal and turnips to some dozen fat bullocks. I was too small to keep out of the muck, and waded through slop and cow-muck until I became absolutely lost. My breeches became so caked in porridge they could have stood upright without me inside them. My hands, by the same process, aided by the raw winds, became so swollen and cracked it was purgatory to wash them. And often I didn't. There was no one interested in whether I washed them or not, and so I degenerated into a 'regular grub-etten little yarker', who cried and grinned, trying to force stiff, hard boots over broken chilblains. I must have looked unkempt and forlorn, but I was perfectly happy. I was too busy to be otherwise, and I always maintain that to be perfectly happy a person should get busy and interested in something.

I made friends with every animal on the farm, and, being young and eager, I used to spend an undue amount of energy making them comfortable and contented, when I might have been taking it easy.

After helping the cowman in the yards, I usually went carting turnips with old Short. I was very proud of old Short, and rode him to the field, sitting sideways on his broad back, to the tune of 'Rosie O'Grady' or 'Irish Molly O'. I was always glad to get into the fields, because – though I liked feeding the beasts – there was the missus's eye peeping at me over the window-curtain as I ran about in the crew-yards, and even when there wasn't any eye to be seen, I always felt it was there somewhere. So I whistled and sang while I filled my cart with turnips and enjoyed the friendship of old Short and Laddie the collie, who always came and threw himself down – when the cart stopped – immediately in front of Short's nose, to the old horse's extreme annoyance.

We went in to dinner at twelve-thirty prompt. The missus was always to the minute with everything – excepting my half-crown, which I will mention later. We had boiled beef for dinner, with vegetables and the never-changing Yorkshire pudding; boiled beef is more economical than roast, and what that lady didn't know about economy wasn't worth learning. I had a little tin mug of ale at dinner, and for a lad who was a staunch teetotaller I got it down very nicely. But, gosh! wasn't it cold swallowing it in winter, fresh drawn from the cellar. George used to say: ' It's a poor belly that can't warm its own beer.'

I generally managed to sit for half an hour over dinner, and then off I had to go chopping kindling, riddling cinders, carrying straw for bedding-down at night, carrying hay into the 'fotherham', filling the chop-bin for the horses, and then, in my spare time, hunt the eggs up. There was no bonus on them now, and – even in the short days of winter – I believe I earned my keep, plus two and six.

We 'bridled-out' at one-thirty, getting back to the stable again – when days were longer at five-thirty. I again milked the four cows, and again I took the milk into the house on the stroke of six. I then had a basin of tea – not over strong – with more fat bacon and plenty of home-made bread and butter. There was plenty of food – good and wholesome – but it never varied until Sunday afternoon, when we had jam or pastry for tea. Only a hungry farm lad could have stuck that regularity – boiled bacon, boiled beef, Yorkshire pudding, boiled bacon, and milk. I looked forward to tea time on Sunday with the eagerness of a child for its Saturday ha'penny.

After tea I fed the calves again, and, to my credit, never spilled the porridge in the straw at night-time. But it's a messy job feeding calves; the little beggars will come fussing round, sucking at your clothes with porridgy mouths, and that is how my clothes came to be so stuck up. After seeing to the calves I helped George in the stable, spending no end of time a-curry-combing and brushing of Short, learning to 'rig-plait' his tail – like the wagoner chaps did for showing – but he never appreciated my efforts to make him look smart, but went on munching his oats as though I didn't exist.

We spent most of our nights in the stable until nine o'clock, when we had a basin of bread and milk, and so to bed. Sometimes other farm lads dropped in for an hour, and other times we walked across to their stables – there being two more farms near to ours. Usually one of them would bring a melodeon, and he was considered a poor gawk who couldn't knock a tune out of a mouth-organ or give a song to pass away the evening. We had rare times in the 'fotherham' seated on the corn-bin or on a truss of hay. Tom fra' Bennett's would strike off with, 'Oh, never go into a sentry-box, to be wrapt in a soldier's cloak', while someone played away on the melodeon. He was a merry sort of lad, was Tom, and his songs always had a spicy flavour. Harry Bates, Farmer Wood's man, always sang sentimental ballads. Harry was a Lincolnshire chap, and their singing, I always noticed, was of a more serious vein than the rollicking Yorkies. His favourite song started with:

A preacher in a village church, one Sunday
   morning said,
Our organist is ill today, will someone play
   instead?

and he would sit on the corn-bin singing as long as you'd a mind to listen. He knew no end of songs as did most of the farm lads – but his were mostly about soldiers sighing for their native 'land' and 'heart-broken lovers', and that sort of stuff, so that as a rule we liked to get Tom singing first. They were all good singers, and good musicians too, and it must not be supposed, because they were farm men and lads, they were just caterwauling. Another diversion, when not singing, was playing dominoes, draughts, or fox-and-geese on the lid of the corn-bin, or seated on the floor with a stable lantern beside us.

Everyone at all the three farms went to bed at nine – though the other two farms allowed their lads until ten on Saturdays – and though it may seem a ridiculous hour to be going to roost, when a man had to be in the fields from six-thirty in the morning he was ready for bed at night. I enjoyed these musical evenings singing old English songs; but alas for the fly in the ointment, if I offered to oblige with 'Hearts of Oak' or some well-known school song, the missus's voice would come from the kitchen door, 'George! George! en yer owt for 'im to do a minute?' and I should be sent to do another odd job.

When we tired of singing, we told tales; at least, the men did – folklore tales – whilst I sat with my ears open, and probably my mouth, taking it all in. If Tom told the story it was all about Yorkshire giants and queer characters who were on friendly terms with the devil; of Lindum Hall (probably Lindholme), where was a barn full of white sparrows; and of a farmer who thought nothing of throwing a plough over his shoulder and carrying it to the field, to save the trouble of hanging on the horse. Of the wonderful feats of strength and enormous appetites of these Yorkshire giants. Of Jimmy Hurst, of Rawcliffe, Doncaster, who went hunting on a bull and wore a hat measuring three yards round the brim. But what I remember best about Jimmy was the ingenious way in which he stopped the sow from lifting the pigsty door off its hinges. He nailed a scythe blade on the bottom of the door.

Strange as they seem, most of these stories were founded on fact, and when Tom finished with his giants, Harry would tell stories of witches. He was a 'Lincy', and his county seemed noted for witches and boggarts. One old witch could turn herself into a hare, and – according to Harry – one day a farmer set his dogs after a hare, which ran into the old witch's cottage. The farmer followed and went into the cottage to claim the hare, but all he saw was the old witch bathing her thigh, which was covered with fresh blood and teeth-marks in exactly the same spot where the dogs had bitten the hare. I'm sure we all believed these tales, as we sat on trusses of hay or on the corn-bin in the 'fotherham', in the dim light of a stable-lantern. Everyone looked very serious and credulous, and if anyone had expressed a doubt about the truth of them, the whole company would have verified the truth by saying, 'I've 'eered my dad tell of 'im mony a time', or 'My grandfeyther ewsed to work on t' varry same plaice.' Indeed it was impossible to doubt; there were so many people who knew these people or 'knew people who knew these people'. It made a great impression on me, especially the witches and boggarts. Whenever I had to go along the dark lane down to the village I thought of them. The conclusion I came to was that Yorkshire was a land of giants and blue-devils, Lincolnshire was overrun with witches and boggarts, and for proper sensible men one must go into Nottinghamshire. For which reason they were called 'Nottingham Lambs'.

Some nights we went sparrow-catching with a riddle fastened to a long hay-fork. We held the riddle on the sides of the stacks or on the ivy where the sparrows roosted on the house-side. I am pleased to say we never found any 'white' sparrows, so evidently we had no 'dealings wi' owd Harry' in our part of the world.

I seldom got down to the village at night, but sometimes I was sent down to get a plough-coulter 'laid', and I always found one or two of my old schoolmates there, on a like errand. The blacksmith was a bit of a politician, and we used to listen with admiration to his political opinions without ever understanding a thing of which he spoke – but wiser folk than us still listen with the same effect. There were always a few lads – and loafers – to be found in the blacksmith's shop at night. 'A rainy day for shoeing horses and a frosty night for plough coulters', would have been a good maxim for the blacksmith, because of the fact that farmers always sent their horses to be shod on a wet day and plough-coulters always needed sharpening when the ground was hard.

One thing I remember very well about my first winter was 'Plough Monday', though I was considered too much of a younker to join in with them; which was as well, for it seemed to me nothing but an ale-gussling affair. Plough Monday – as perhaps you know – falls on the first Monday in Epiphany, and marks the end of the Christmas festivities, when the plough is supposed to start fallowing down for the winter. Well, that winter everyone was forrard wi' the ploughing, having had an open back-end, and I believe it was Tom fra' Bennett's who conceived the idea of reviving Plough Monday. It was a custom more honoured in the breach than the observance, and was, even at that time, dying out. But Tom was a regular Yorkshire dale-man, always ready for a spree of any sort. So a lot of them made 'one yoke' on Plough Monday, that is, working until two o'clock instead of coming home for dinner and 'yoking out' again, and spent the afternoon cleaning up a plough and decorating it with caddis and rosettes.

After tea they dragged the plough round the village, singing at all the big houses and such as were likely to give them ale money. They did very well at it, too, for the plough was left in the yard at the Black Swan for several days, as none of the party were capable of trailing it home again for several nights. They had a particular song for this occasion, the last two lines of each verse ending with:

We've ploughed a fair acre, I swear and I
   vow.
We're all jolly fellows that follow the plough!

And they were jolly, too; though anyone trailing a plough on the highway nowadays would be locked up, and serve them right, too.

When the snow came we used to go sleighing down the mill field, which had a steep run of several hundred yards. It was jolly fun whizzing down to the bottom, and having to roll off into the snow because the track had frozen so hard we couldn't pull up without plunging into the stream. All the village turned out to sleigh, or to watch others go speeding down the slope, for the older folk, whose sleighing days were over, couldn't resist the pleasure of watching lads and lassies all in a mix-up, floundering in the deep snow at the bottom of the track. And didn't the girls enjoy it too, half a dozen lads and girls riding on a sleigh that was only meant to hold three, laughing and squealing, while the stars twinkled over the fir trees, and the mill dam crinkled and chinked as the frost gripped tighter and tighter on its over-flush. No doubt many village romances started on the sleigh track, but I was too young then to bother about such daftness.

The snow lasted more than a week on this occasion, and I enjoyed a bit of ease in the day-time. When it snowed, I sawed logs under the cart-shed, and when the snow stopped coming down we all set in to manure-leading, getting all the yards cleaned out before the snow had gone. Then we just dodged about, seeing to the cattle, and even my odd jobs came to a standstill.

After the snow had gone I had to go ploughing the turnip ground, where the sheep had been feeding. I took Flower and Short, and felt mightily important at being trusted with the young mare. I had nothing to feel conceited about, however, for the spell of bad weather had made my hands more cracked than ever, while the raw thaw wind turned them blue with cold. My overcoat was tied round with string in place of buttons, an important part of my breeches had worn through with riding on old Short's rough cart-saddle, while a trellis-work of binder-twine did service for buckles on my leggings. I was still a 'bit of a yarker', not much higher than the plough-ails, and two women coming along the lane stopped to look as I turned on the headland. They watched me struggling to ease the plough into position, and, as they turned to go, I heard one of them remark: 'Aye! He's som'dys poor bairn!'

I felt a bit nettled, and more than a bit ashamed of my appearance, while the importance of being allowed to drive the young mare completely vanished. I had become a little ragamuffin, and knew if I presented myself at home in that state I should cop it. The reason they never knew was because I never went home except on Sunday night, when I was respectable; though I kept my hands out of sight as much as possible and spent a torturous time trying to get them clean before I went.

Why I seldom went to the village or home on Saturday was this: in the first place, Saturday was as long and busy as any other day in wintertime, and didn't allow of much time off, but the main reason was my half-crown per week. The missus had agreed to pay me every Saturday night, and for several weeks I went home with my half-crown. Then she began to have no change and deferred payment until 'next week', till it became a regular thing, and ended in one-sided arguments on how many weeks were due before I could have a draw.

I would mention it to Harry, the cowman, first, as we sat eating our 'forenoon drinkings' after feeding the cattle. I would say to him, 'She hasn't paid me again this week!' and Harry would say, 'She's a —bargas' and kid me to 'stick up for thi sen', and 'don't thee be shoved off.' Thus encouraged I screwed up enough courage when Saturday night came to ask: 'Have you any change this week, please? I should like to walk down home tonight.'

'I'll see what change I've getten. How much does ta want?'

'It's five weeks now, I think.'

'Five wicks! Yar young blaggard, I'll gie ye five wicks, comin' 'ere wi' a tale like that!' and she would glare at me, with her tall bony figure towering over me like a hawk over a sparrow.

But I stuck up to her, maintaining my 'five weeks', while according to her reckoning it was 'only three', and in the end she would split the difference, so that I generally got diddled out of half a crown in the course of five or six weeks. She was a rare old bird, to be sure.

Now, when I heard those two women talk pityingly about my appearance, I felt nettled about it, and ashamed, for I had always been brought up to be clean and tidy, and my only excuse is I was only a nipper and hadn't bothered. So that night, while George saw to the horses, I sat in the 'fother-ham' with my breeches over my knees, gathering up the fragments – it was a blessing we had no visitors that night. I made poor progress, for it's an awkward job handling a needle with cracked hands, and when bedtime came I decided to carry on upstairs. The missus decided differently, and just as I was sliding upstairs she called me back, saying: 'Let me look at them 'ands!'

I showed her my hands, and she, taking me by the scruff, marched me up to the sink, saying: 'Nay tha doesna', tha doesna' gan 'tween my sheets wi' paws like them!' and she made me wash and scrub them while I was ready to howl with pain.

Then she poured glycerine over them, and, lending me a pair of old gloves so as not to grease the sheets, said: 'Theer! git!' So I 'got'. Next morning I found my clothes neatly mended, and my hands nearly better. I wondered, after, if those women had called on her. I never let my hands get bad again, and Harry advised me to dry them with 'fine sharps' after dabbling about with pigswill, so life got more pleasant on the axiom: 'A stitch in time'.

On Friday mornings I took a load of corn to be ground at the mill, bringing the load back I had taken on the previous Friday. It was interesting to watch the miller starting up the big waterwheel, with its 'thump, thump' as the water came pouring into the buckets, and the big stones turning slowly round as they ground our corn into meal. Watermills are now out of date, most farmers having a petrol engine and a mill of their own, and, though they don't grind as good as the stones did, it no doubt saves a deal of time, while the miller cannot now be charged with having diddled them.

The miller was generally suspected of having pinched a few pounds of meal from each sack, it being the custom to deduct so many pounds from each sack of grain as being 'lost in the stones'. Whether it was all lost or not, the miller's horse and cattle were always sleeker and fatter than anyone's, though he grew no corn of his own.

One thing the old lady was queer about was her pigs, and someone had to sit up and watch whenever a sow was farrowing. I remember going into supper one night, and the missus saying: 'T' old sow's a bit unasy tonight. When ye 've had yer bit o' supper yer can sit wi' 'er a while.'

So she gave me a stool to sit on, promising to take me off in an hour's time if the event hadn't come off. It was warm and stuffy in the loose-box where the sow was lying in, and, having nothing to look at but a big, hefty black-and-white sow, I soon nodded off. I was awakened by a smart clap across the ear, and, being but half-awake, the place seemed full of little pigs, and there stood the missus, carrying on something alarming because I had neglected my work. I was feeling sleepy and cross, and picked up the stool as though to throw it at someone; perhaps I might have done, but just then the sow gave an angry 'woof' and hustled us outside. I was never asked to sit up at a sow's lying-in again.

On Sunday morning we got up at six and had breakfast at seven. It was still 'fat boiled' same as other days, though we often had coffee in place of milk. After feeding all the animals and seeing that everything was made comfortable, we walked round the fields until noon.

Every Sunday morning a group of farm chaps could be seen examining each other's ploughing, for ploughing was a fine art in those days, and the plough lads took great pride in showing off their best. It was the introduction of American diggers that killed their interest, for ploughing has no glory when done by a digger plough. Lots of good ploughmen refused to get hired to a place where diggers were used, and so drifted to town work, not because of higher pay, but because they could no longer put heart or art into their work. Digger ploughs and dutch barns – in their earlier days – drove as many good men off the land as did lower wages.

And so we spent our Sunday mornings criticizing each other's work, though George seldom went off our own farm. We used to walk round with the gun, and Laddie following on behind. Sometimes a stoat or a weasel would run in the plantation hedge, and Laddie would get busy trying to get him out of the briars, presently to come scampering after us on three legs, and his coat stuck-up with burdocks. While I was taking the thorn out of his foot, he would lick my face and whine and then scamper off for fresh adventure. What I liked best about our fields was the wide view; being on top of a steep hill, you could see – from the 'far Brecks' – into Lincolnshire and Nottinghamshire, woods and squares of fields lying right away until they became lost in the mistiness of space. Our fields, too, had a wild and rugged sort of loveliness about them. The land was thin and craggy, and, I suppose, required thin and craggy folk to make a living out of it. The rock was limestone, and in places showed through the soil, like the bare bones of a mammoth skeleton. These knolls and patches were left unploughed, and short, stunted thorns and whins had taken root in the crevices; so that, while it hadn't the luxuriant beauty of the lower parkland, it had a more natural beauty of its own.

I mustn't forget one important piece of business which took place on Sunday morning. None of these little villages possessed a barber's shop – heads were too few for a barber to make a living out of them – so hair-cutting was a spare-time occupation, reserved for Sunday morning. The shepherd was chief barber, though often a coachman or groom would set up with horse clippers. John Henry was the most popular barber in our village, and he was a shepherd. His backyard was strewn with human hair on warm Sunday mornings; on cold or wet days the hair fell on Mrs John Henry's kitchen floor. You had your choice, too, 'Shears or scissors?' for he cut equally well with either; but denounced 'these 'ere 'orse clippers; don't make no sort of a job of it; they seam it and sear it!' he would say, and in his opinion there was nothing to beat a pair of long-pointed sheep-shears for the 'nick o' the neck' and 'back o' the years'. Whenever I called I was always careful to say, 'Scissors, please!' for I didn't like the look of his long-pointed shears.

I spent Sunday afternoon – along with the other lads – catching sparrows, or rat-hunting, or digesting the week's news in the local paper, sitting in some stable or saddle-room. Maybe some lad would have a copy of the *Police News* – a terrible paper it was – or the *Red Letter* or *Ally Sloper*. So we got sensation, entertainment, or jollification; but never a line of good reading, for which I longed. I was too timid to bring my school-prizes out for the other lads to jeer at, for I knew Lady Brassey, Captain Marryat, Charles Lever, or my book of poetry, would be considered 'rammel', and probably they would get roughly handled in my present company. So I shut myself out of the world of books and hunted rats. It was only in winter that we spent Sunday afternoon loafing around the buildings; in summer we went birds' nesting, raiding orchards, or nutting. It just depended on the time of year. Some of the lads were the fortunate owners of cycles, going long rides for the day.

We had tea at five o'clock on Sundays, which I always looked forward to on account of the jam. This was a welcome change to a lad of fourteen after six days of bacon and milk. After tea I went to church or chapel; I liked chapel best because it loosed half an hour earlier than did church.

Sometimes I spent the evening by our fire at home. Most farm lads passed Sunday evening at the street corner, while the wagoners and seconders were to be found in the Black Swan or the Jug and Glass. Had I lived farther from home I might have followed their course, but mother insisted on my going to church, for which I am now truly thankful.

I couldn't help contrasting our cheerful fire and cosy kitchen, with its threadbare carpet and the dresser loaded with books and ornaments, against the big, cheerless farm kitchen, where no one seemed at ease excepting Laddie, who occupied most of the hearthrug as his just dues. But I never let on about it, and told the little ones how well I was doing, and what a fine horse was old Short; and mother would smile and say: 'Aye! It's all very well having a fine horse, but she doesn't seem in a hurry with that back-money.'

One Sunday night I had a pleasant surprise. It was the time of year when nights put out, with spring not far behind. We were in a clothing-club, run by the schoolmistress, and when I called in home there was a pair of breeches and a pair of leggings waiting for me. The club had paid out. It seems a trifling matter to write about now, but for a lad getting half a crown a week it was an event of great importance. Mother said: 'I've made a "put" to get you these all winter, for I'm sure those you're wearing must be threadbare by now!'

Poor mother! If she'd have seen 'em, wouldn't she have carried on, and me brought up respectable. So I just gave her a hug and said, 'They were about done for!' and felt mightily proud, because now I could be neatly dressed in corduroy breeches and leggings and stride it out like a full-blown wagoner.

Five

THE RAILWAY

So I GOT THROUGH my first winter as a hired lad, and, though the passage was rough at times, on the whole there was nothing to grumble about. I was interested in my work, and that helps a lot, especially for a young lad living isolated from the village. I had the idea that the well-being of some twenty head of cattle depended on my constant care. So I looked on the cattle as my own, gave them their hay at supper-time – the cowman finished at five-thirty – and walked round all the sheds, making everything comfortable for the night, with an air of proprietorship.

Then – the change seemed all of a sudden – the spring came, and the cattle were turned out to grass; and, instead of having to help the cowman, I now 'yoked-out' at six-thirty with a pair of horses. It was glorious to be out in the fields all day, away from the missus's eye peeping over the window-curtain. I was dressed respectable once again; my hands were clean and free from cracks, and I found harrowing for spring corn a jolly life, with the sun shining on both sides of the hedges. I sang 'Farmer's Boy', 'Bonnie Dundee' or whatever song came uppermost – for farmer-boys knew heaps of good songs – and watched the sun go chasing shadows across the fields like troops of wild horses. I watched them go rolling along, over the hedge, and over the next, and career merrily away up Mill Wood side. The wind played with my coat lappets, tossed Flower's thick mane in a ruffled mat to the wrong side of her neck, and toppled the peewits head over tail as they swirled and screamed over the horses' heads.

It was like as if winter had never been, and it was always springtime, with merry winds and warm sun that played with the foal-foot and dandelion, and danced a polka with a crowd of frivolous lambs around the humps and hollows of an old Danish battlefield.

According to the missus, I had done no work all winter. 'Not till corn-sowing does a lad addle his keep, let alone his bit o' brass!' she said. Be that as it may, I found harrowing corn less tiring than carrying skeps of turnips.

I found, however, that as the days lengthened, my odd jobs strengthened. Several clutches of chicks came off, and when I went into dinner the missus would say: 'Ere yar, jist nip wi' this rice an' a can o' watter while I sarve thi puddin'.'

So I ran and nipped round some dozen coops while my pudding was making its way platewards. At night I nipped again – before long there were twenty coops – feeding chicks and coaxing the wakeful ones to go to bed. I was busy from teatime to bedtime, with occasionally an hour's cricket or tip-cat with the other farm lads on the bit of green by Bennett's cart-shed. But to tell the truth, I enjoyed looking after things better than playing games, and, as I ran about, with Laddie trotting behind, I always visualised a day coming when I should have a little place of my own, with a horse like old Short and a dog like Laddie.

One night in early summer we had quite an exciting time, rook-shooting. The rookery was in the wood on Bennett's farm, and after the squire had had his day's sport among them he allowed the farm chaps to have an hour at night. Though there were not many young rooks left, the sport was great just the same. George and the 'seconder' from Bennett's and Wood's wagoner carried guns, while we nippers had to scrim up the trees to dislodge any rooks that got stuck in the branches. We had an alarming five minutes, too, and were thankful when what looked liked a serious accident could be treated lightly; though young Bobby fra' Wood's never could see the fun of it.

It happened like this. The few young rooks that were left kept pretty near the nests and took some potting, so, with a ladder reared to the first boughs, we lads were sent up the trees to poke them out. We were enjoying the fun very nicely, when Bennett's 'seconder', a bit over-eager, fired up the tree, and the next thing we saw was young Bobby swaying up and down on the lower branches. We felt sure he had been shot by the way he came crashing down, and he only escaped a broken neck by being held up on the lower branches. He looked in a nice pickle to be sure, and being a fat, red-faced little lad, looked quite comical as he swayed gently up and down, caught by one leg on the bending twigs, and clawing the air like a puppy held up by the tail. He was just out of reach, and looked like falling on his head before the ladder could be reared.

He was not shot, as we at first feared, but the gun had startled him, causing him to overbalance; so George, seeing things were no worse, cuffed the seconder a rare wallock on the side of the head and boot-toed him into the bargain. Now, it is one thing to boot-toe the 'lad', but quite a different matter to boot-toe a second-horseman, and he, being a chap of some twenty years, felt a bit hurt about it. We just missed enjoying a splendid scrap between George and Alf because Farmer Bennett came on the scene to see if we were having any luck. We all wished he hadn't come, but we all agreed with his verdict: 'That it's not the thing to shoot up a tree while a lad's in it.'

In May, George clipped our small flock of sheep; it not being a large enough flock to warrant sending for the man who went round sheep-shearing. It was then I clipped my first sheep – just to get my hand in – and it was done in my spare time at night as a matter of course. The ewe I practised my skill on was a very ancient Wensleydale, with not much go in it, and fairly straight in the wool. Before I had finished, the old ewe was all go and the wool anything but straight. I struggled and sweated with that sheep for a good hour – it took George about ten minutes to clip a sheep – and when I had finished I felt really sorry for the old ewe. No wonder she kicked; I had nicked the skin in several places and she looked a sorry object when at last I let her go. It would have been much nicer, both for the ewe and myself, if George had shown me how by helping, but that was never done; it spoiled a lad to be helped, so I just watched how he did it, and then – it was rather rough on the sheep.

I was very busy, too, in lambing time – but that was earlier on – and I felt mighty important when I brought my first pair of lambs into the world. We kept the in-lamb ewes in the barn at night, putting them in empty stalls in the cowsheds or in loose boxes as they lambed. I remember going to look round one night before going to bed, and finding one of the 'massams' in difficulties. Instead of fetching George, as I had been told to do, I offed with my coat, rolled up my sleeves, and assisted two lambs into the world. The missus gave me sixpence, saying I were 'gettin' a rare lad'. The sixpence came as a great surprise, for she was not over good at giving tips.

During lambing time I had two 'caed' lambs added to my list of odd jobs, and, while I was proud of them at first, I am afraid I hated the sight of them before summer was out. Like Mary's little lamb, they followed me everywhere, such a 'ma-a-ing' and 'ba-a-ing' you never heard whenever I spoke or came in sight. It seems very nice having a pet lamb to fuss around, but unless you fasten them in somewhere, and securely too, they become a nuisance. Sometimes I would be going down to the village on Sunday night, thinking I had escaped them nicely, when all at once would come that 'maa-a, maa-a-a', and the little beggars would come helter-skelter down the road, with their tails swinging round and round as though fastened on with a swivel. If I was well ahead I ran like blazes, but usually it was hopeless, and I had to turn back, saying things about lambs not to be found in the Book of Common Prayer. So I fastened them in the yard and ran to church.

My summer at Hill-top passed very pleasantly, and I believe I learned quite a lot under George's tutoring. He was a good all-round man, and I owe him thanks for letting me have a go at almost every job that turned up, and, I must add, there isn't another class of work that requires so many different kinds of skill from one man as farming.

I drove the grass-reaper in haytime; swung the scythe, in turn with Harry, when opening out the corn; and built a barley stack in harvest – only a small one, and it needed a whole row of props on the teeming side to keep it upright.

With all this, however, I became dissatisfied. Although I liked the work, I wasn't making my fortune quick enough, and the reason for my change of views came through Soldier George. If he had another name, I never heard of it; to everyone he was just 'Sojer' George, and I came to know him while he was striking mangolds in the ten-acre. I was horse-hoeing in front of him, and as we sat having 'drinkings' in the hedge-bottom he would tell me wonderful yarns about his soldiering days, and always ended by saying: 'Sojerin's the life for a young lad', and advised me to take the – he always called it – queen's shilling.

He was a tall, straight, brown-skinned old chap, not overstout, with a snow-white military moustache that swept in graceful curves from ear to ear, and as I listened, and watched him twist and twirl that magnificent 'tache, he became my hero, and I swallowed every word he said as though it was gospel.

According to what he told me, he had been a farm lad, and had run away at the age of fifteen after being thrashed by an angry farmer. He had taken the queen's shilling at Pontefract, and saw his first engagement at Alma. Though I should be inclined to doubt some of his exploits now, in those days I believed every word he said, and, anyhow, he was the most interesting and intelligent person I had ever met, having started his career in the Crimea and got his discharge after the Boxer rising.

My imagination was so fired with his account of the free-and-easy life, that I could talk of nothing else but soldiering when I went down home. I told mother I wanted to be a soldier, and had she disagreed with my notion I am sure I should have packed up and gone. But she didn't say a word contrary to my going; all she said was: 'Well, if you're set on going, you'll be like to go. The Lord has provided so far, and I'm not one to stand i' the light of my only son, so wi' God's help we shall manage – somehow.'

I felt mean and selfish after that way of putting it. I felt more like a deserter than a valiant soldier, so I let the fit wear off. And since then it has never been my luck to wander far from the sight of my own chimney-smoke. But he was a fine old chap was 'Sojer' George, always looked spick and span no matter what he was doing, and I only hope he sometimes found as ready a listener as I was; which is doubtful, for most people just scoffed at him.

Another thing that made me restless during this year was of a very startling nature, proving very eventful to quite a number of little villages in the West Riding – or South Yorkshire, as the colliers have it. For several years there had been rumours of a railroad coming through Little Norwood – the village where I lived – but no one really believed it. (Little Norwood, by the way, is not so spelled in any guide book or map.) The village lay in a valley surrounded by hills and woods, and on the road to nowhere in particular, so it seemed the most unlikely place to be disturbed by a railtrack. However, that springtime the long-talked-of railroad became a fact, and our village became a place of some importance.

First of all trial-holes were made across the fields to determine the nature of the cuttings. Blasting sand rumblings disturbed the quiet of the hills, and Little Norwood sat up and took notice. It caused a great upheaval all along its track, for never again were these quiet villages and farmsteads to settle down to their former peaceful ways, and this rural part of the West Riding developed into the South Yorkshire coalfield.

But it started with the railway; a light railroad was laid down first, running uphill and down like a long shiny snake across the fields, splitting them into sections, leaving odd comers here and narrow strips there, to the inconvenience of the farmers, causing them to make roundabout journeys to reach the remains of fields that had formerly been on the doorstep. It was no respecter of persons either, and encroached itself on the privacy of country houses or ran over the corners of farm buildings.

Then a loco came, fussing and snorting like some prehistoric monster, scattering the sheep and cattle from their grazing. It brought behind it engine-sheds and fitting-shops, so that the miller's field, which had once been a sanctuary for birds, rang all day with the clatter and bang of hammers and the snorting of steam-engines. It came one day with a whole town of tin – at least, it was called Tin Town, though most of it was made of wood – and it brought in a strange race of people, who taught us new ways and habits. They married and intermixed with the natives, so that in a few years you couldn't tell a Norwood yeoman from an alien.

It wasn't the settled inhabitants of Tin Town, so much as the nomadic race of navvies, that shook the villages to their very foundations. A paternal government had not then docketed and labelled each workman with a labour card. They just came and went, hundreds of them; where to, or where from, nobody knew nor cared, and the quiet country lanes became infested with as scurvy a lot of weary willies as ever got bitten with a louse.

So lost were they, even their names were hidden, and they wandered about under such labels as 'Scotty', 'Yorkey', 'Lincoln', 'Brum', 'Bedford' and 'ole Glorster'. A thin man would be 'Slen', and a fat one – poor beggars, they were very scarce – 'Nobby'; but generally they were called after the town or country that had given them birth. Much beer and blood began to flow in the street on Saturday nights and Sundays. Drunken brawls, revellings and revilings, drink-sodden navvies sprawling in the gutter, tramps sleeping in barns, tramps threatening timid housewives for a crust, and tramps massaging their stinking feet at the village drinking trough in defiance of the notice which said: 'This water is used for drinking purposes, and must not be polluted. By Order.'

Never since the time of the Danes had our village suffered such an invasion. Hen-roosts were rifled, orchards robbed and private enclosures raided with impunity. As happy-go-lucky, beer-swilling, God-forsaken a race as ever sought for a job and hoped not to find one. What a change it was in our little village where everyone had known everybody, and it wasn't safe to speak slightingly of one man to another for fear they should be second cousins at least. But it affected no one so much as Mr Ounceby, our chief grocer. He was church warden and overseer too, and the shocks he received during that summer caused him to retire from business. It had its amusing side, too, according to the many tales that got about concerning our grocer and his dealings with vagrant navvies. For a matter of thirty years he had run his business in his own way, no one daring to question so honourable a gentleman about his prices, nor point out to him the fact that he sold his thumb with every purchase. But the navvies had no such scruples, and Mr Ounceby, in black alpaca coat and white dickie, got the shock of his life when in walked a big, lumbering navvy, demanded, 'Half a-nounce o' twist, guv'nor!' and, as Mr Ounceby's gentlemanly thumb touched the scale, bawled out, 'Weigh that again, guv'nor, weigh that again, and keep yer b— thumb off this time!'

It was terrible for the dignity of Mr Ounceby, and he did the only thing possible, he retired, to the benefit of all housewives with slender purses.

So the coming of the railroad did a certain amount of good, if it only adjusted weights and measures. But it did more. Not all the navvies were drunks and wasters; lots of them, in fact, were hard-working, steady-going fellows, and Little Norwood was not slow to take advantage. As I have already mentioned, the village was much frequented by tourists, and nearly every cottage bore the card: 'Teas Provided'. Well, Little Norwood took down its cards with 'Teas Provided', and put up other cards bearing the inscription 'Lodgings', and everyone with a spare bed, and many who hadn't a bed worth mentioning, went in for lodgers. It was the gold rush for Little Norwood, never before had it seen so many golden sovereigns waiting to be picked up, and it made the most of its chances.

There was the inevitable overcrowding; sanitation was unheard of, and district officers of health were as yet unborn; but Little Norwood cared not for these things. It overcrowded and fought and reaped its strange harvest. But it lost its rurality, and progressed and expanded until now it has produced urban houses and is a thriving village in the South Yorkshire coalfield, with a woefully long list of unemployed.

One thing I could never understand was the fuss and palaver which arose between our common-holders and the railroad contractors. The railroad took about one acre of bracken and gorse of our common; it was useless land for grazing and would have starved a donkey to death. But these old commoners arose tooth and nail, and defended their rights so well that a corresponding portion of rich meadowland was given them on the far side of the common for what the railway had taken on this side.

For a time the paper for our district was full of 'Commoners', and the street corners buzzed with excitement, 'Settlements', 'Enclosures', 'Parish Records', and 'what their feythers and the Lord of the Manor put their hands to i' the thirty-sixes', all of which I could make nothing of at the time, but now, hats off to the commoners of Little Norwood, for I find they fared bravely and well during the 'Enclosure', and retained their rights, while each steading was granted an acre of allotment.

I have mentioned the railroad at some length because it was the railroad that put many of these little villages on the map and transformed this unknown quarter of the West Riding into a hive of industry, the South Yorkshire coalfield. So it came about that two things – for a time – turned my thoughts away from farm work. First, old Soldier George, with his wonderful tales, then the still more wonderful tales of money to be picked up on the railroad. And I wondered, was this where I made a fortune? However, I couldn't leave before Martlemas, being bound with a 'Fastening penny' to stay the twelvemonth. Before November came the missus had become quite friendly and affable, so, having no man to advise me on the matter, I allowed myself to be persuaded into stopping-on again. And though I did go on the railroad eventually, it was only for a short while, the reason for which I shall mention later.

Six

MARTLEMAS FAIR

A<small>T</small> MARTLEMAS I had my week's holiday, and on Martlemas Saturday went to the hiring fair at Doncaster, and as near as I remember this was the order of our going.

Ben Cobb, the carrier, was due to start at nine a.m. At nine-thirty he led out old Jasper and hitched him in the wagon shafts. He was never less than half an hour late at any time, so we reckoned we were making a good start. Old Bob Dale, by virtue of his years, sat at the front on the right-hand side. This was a great concession when travelling in a covered wagon because the interior was in semi-darkness. From this vantage point he described the state of the country as viewed over Ben Cobb's rounded shoulders. By his side sat Martha, his wife, who hid under the seat a large butter-basket in which reposed Owd Bob's concertina. Next to Martha sat John Henry English and his wife, Lizzie. He, you will remember, was shepherd to Mr Merril, and chief barber to the village. He was a tall, lean old man, and looked rather like a picture I had seen of William Wordsworth. Next to Lizzie sat two servant-girls, Elsie and Doris, and that made up the right-hand side. Seated on the front-board, alongside old Ben, was William Bonner, a little, dark-haired man with black side-whiskers; he carried on his knee a melodeon wrapped carefully in a large spotted neckerchief. Next came our cowman, Harry Butterfield, and Mary, his wife, who also had a shopping basket, in which lay Harry's melodeon. Next to Mary sat Ernest Gill, a groom, wearing very loud check riding-breeches, and looking altogether out of place in this more soberly clad community. Ernest was single and clean-shaven, but a constant application of snuffle and ale had given his countenance such varying degrees of blue and red that a pair of flowing whiskers would have greatly improved his features. However, he was a rare hand on the tin whistle and a good singer when not 'ower far gone', so that his company was always welcome where anything was going forward.

Next to Ernest was Harry Butterfield junior, aged thirteen years, whom Harry senior was taking to be hired, saying: 'It's time he put his feet under som'dy else's table.' Bob fra' Bennett's and Sam fra' Wood's, along with myself, were squeezed in at the back, and, old Ben having packed under the seats various articles and hampers – which sawed into our legs with every jolt and roll of the wagon – we started on our journey.

In one thing could the carrier's cart beat the modern bus, and that was in the variety of smells. There was tarpaulin over all; then came leather, then apples and cow-cake, with occasionally a calf or a crate of chickens. We lurched and rolled steadily along, without much thought of time or speed, until we entered the first village on the road to town, where old Jasper, the blue-roan horse, drew up from force of habit in front of the Little Brown Jug.

Here most of the party got down for a 'livener', and when they got up again were certainly enlivened. From being polite and formal during the first two miles, they were now quite chatty and eloquent; the women especially, confiding to each other their own family secrets. As we passed Church-house Farm in this village it started old Bob to tell the story of Farmer Westby, who lived there when Bob was a youth.

'Aye! he wer' a rare sort!' began Bob as we rolled and bumped among the scents of the wagon. 'Every October, at his first threshing o' wheat, he put the copper on and "cree'd" his first bushel of new wheat to mak' frummity.'

'And gie'd it to the poor, didn't 'e. Bob?' asked John Henry, leaning forward.'

'Aye! he did that theer. When I lived in wi' him, I remember ther' ewsed to be twelve wooden bowls set out on t' side-table, and whomsoever 'ed a mind could coom an' sample his first takkin' o' wheat!'

'An' what blinkin' good might that do, d'yer reckon?' broke in Ernest with a sneer.

'Nivver thee mind, lad,' answered Bob, getting a bit warm; 'tha dosna' know tha'rt born yit!' And turning to the rest of the company, said confidingly: 'It wer' a nowald custom, handed down from his feyther's time. Things wer' mighty bad then, I reckon, i' what he ewsed to call the "'ungry forties"; he ewsed to tell us 'ow wheat got to 'undred shillin's a quarter, and t' farm labourers wer' jist deein' off wi' starvation. His feyther was a good-'earted chap – and soa was his son, my maister – an' 'e 'ed that pity like he cree'd 'em a bushel o' wheat ivery week till times come better.'

'An' 'e kep' it up, seemly?' broke in Mrs English.

'An' 'e kep' it up!' answered Bob. 'An' wer' so compassionated, 'e vowed to give his first 'elpin' o' wheat to the poor sa long as 'e farmed Church-house Farm. An' that's 'ow frummity day cum about!' he ended, looking defiantly at the groom.

Everybody acclaimed the Westbys as being rare folk, and after listening to old Jasper's steady clamp-clamp for a minute, someone said: 'Nah, Bob, has ta brought t' owd concertina?'

Bob nodded at Martha, and Martha rummaged under the seat, upsetting everybody's basket but her own, and rose again, breathless but triumphant, with old Bob's concertina. Bob opened out with 'An Old Man gazed on a Photography' and by the time the chorus was reached, two melodeons, two mouth-organs, a tin whistle and a mixed choir had joined in:

Two little girls in blue, lads.
Two little girls in blue.
They were sisters and we were brothers.
We learned to love the two.

The covered wagon became a musical-box on wheels, and old Jasper, unused to such junketings, broke into a trot and beat time for the musicians with a clop-clop-clop on the hard road. When that was ended, Ernest Gill

– to seek favour for his former lapse – sang about a lady who 'shot the squire, on the banks of the sweet Dundee.' He was warmly clapped at the end, and after giving us 'Two Lovely Black Eyes' we found old Jasper had drawn into the Black Lion yard of the next village.

Everyone got out here, for it's thirsty work singing in a carrier's wagon, and after refreshing ourselves with a pint all round, we loaded up again merrier than ever.

'Did yer ever 'ear,' began John Henry, when we had got settled down again, 'about the performin' bears what ewsed to put up at the Black Lion?'

Everyone had heard it a dozen times at least, but no one said so; so, while the wagon swayed and rocked to the jingle of harness, the clamp-clamp of old Jasper, and the lingering smell of tarpaulin, leather, and cow-cake, John Henry got on with his story.

'It wer' when I wer' a ewth,' he continued. 'There ewsed to be a couple o' chaps come round wiv a dancin' bear.'

'Yer said performin' bear, afore!' broke in Ernest, who was immediately pulled up by Mrs Butterfield remarking: 'Tell yer what, young man, yer've ta much o' that what cat licks its hind wi'.'

Ernest being properly snubbed, John Henry made another start. 'Bill Munday kept the Black Lion then – '

''E does nah!' rudely interrupted Ernest, the groom.

'He wer' this Bill Munday's father, tha foil!' continued John Henry, while we all glared savagely at the hapless Ernest, 'an' he kep' the bit o' medder that runs wi' the place. He did a bit o' cattle-dealing an' all, an' one day – soa the tale goes – he sold a calver to a chap fra' Tickleby. Apparently, when he went to Bill's for his cow, she'd just calved, so 'e couldn't tak' 'er away, and Bill and him got to arguin' as to who should 'ev the calf, the long and short of it being, this chap decided to come back wi' the spring-cart and smuggle the calf awa' while Bill wa' busy wi' his customers. They wer' both a bit cute, and suspicious-like of each other, so whether Bill wer' to blame for what 'appened I doan't know; but that neet, who should pull up but these two chaps wi' the performin' bear, so Bill 'e moves the calf out o'

the calf-pen to accommodate the bear. When all wer' quiet at neet, an' Bill
wer' busy in the pub, up drives this 'ere bloke fra' Tickleby, come to bag
the calf. He dursn't show a light for fear o' bein' seen, so goes pottering
in wi' a bag among the straw where he had last seen the calf. He groped
about i' the dark until he felt what seemed like the calf, and then pulled.
Lucky for him the bear wer' chained up, and ony gev' 'im a clout aside o'
his yed what knocked him soft for a minnit. When 'e cum round, there 'e
saw two starin' eyes glarin' at 'im an' sich a snadin' an' rattlin' o' chains,
he thought for sure it wer' the devil come for 'im, an' gev' a fearsome yell
what brought out all the house to see what wer' the matter. After that, he
wer' allus chaffed at an' spoken of as the man who tried to bag a bear!'

When John Henry had finished his story, Ernest Gill was heard to
remark, 'Tha' can tell a good tale, can ta' whistle?' which seemed like
causing some disharmony in the company, so we lads and lassies at the
back struck up with:

> Just like the ivy on the old garden wall.
> Clinging so tightly what'er befall.
> As you grow older I'll be constant and true.
> Just like the i-evy I cling to you,

which had the effect of restoring harmony, and Bill Bonner, on the front-
board, gave his contribution by singing and playing on his melodeon a
rollicking air, with this refrain:

> For I'm barn ta begin an' alter mi waire
> Am gerrin' sa thin an' sa pairl,
> Fo arl nivver get fowertin dairs na moer
> I' Waekfield Jairl.

It was a rattling chorus, which lasted us into Doncaster, when the music
stopped on account of the impossibility of singing or playing with the iron
tyres bumping over the stone setts. I ought to have told you. Bill Bonner was
a 'Yorkey', like Tom fra' Bennett's, and, like him, was fall of merry songs.
Tom and Farmer Wood's man, of course, were not with us, having gone on

their Martlemas week, one to Lincolnshire and one to Driffield, near York.

And so old Jasper drew us into the marketplace alongside other carriers' carts from miles around, and the smell of tarpaulin, leather, cow-cake, apples, calves, pigs and poultry became more pronounced than ever. It was the annual hiring or 'stattis' (statutes) for farm servants from South Yorkshire, North Notts, North Lincolnshire and a small portion of Derby, and represented the biggest babel of dialects since the time of Noah. The streets were crowded with farm chaps seeking new masters, and all were dressed in breeches and leggings, while most of them wore favours in their caps, such as one gets by throwing at Aunt Sallies, and, on account of the pubs being open all day, many of them had obtained a staggering gait at an early hour. There were fightings and uproars, embracings of old friends and introductions to new ones, for you must bear in mind these lads had known no holiday for a twelvemonth, and were now let loose with a purse full of golden sovereigns.

It was an interesting crowd, and you could pick out the Lincolnshire 'fenners' by their fancy for bright blue cords, set off with as many pearl buttons as could be conveniently carried on a pair of breeches and leggings. They were usually of heavier build than the 'woadies' (men from the Yorkshire and Lincolnshire wolds), being of the broad, chubby kind, while the 'woadies' were tall, raw-boned, and straight on the leg. The 'Yorkeys', too, often wore carters' smocks, with a whip hanging over their necks; so a farmer could guess pretty nearly what district a would-be hireling came from. But the dialect was the surest indicator, and if you listened a moment you might hear something like this:

YORK. Worroh, Bill! 'Ow beesta?
LINCOLN. Fair-ta mid! 'Owby yar?
YORK. Gradely foine! Stoppin' agin?
LINCOLN. Neah! Oor maister's ower fratchy!
YORK. Nuff-tate?
LINCOLN. Clairkenbairken on a blue-edge plairt, mairt!
YORK. Ugh! Atta barm darn tarn?
LINCOLN. Lairter. Cansta feyther a noddum?

YORK. Yor, lad! A lyle slap i' a milk piggin' for oi!
LINCOLN. Weel, com thi' wairs!

And so you heard the sharps and flats of the dialect scale and were able to distinguish thereby what part of the shires he came from.

We three lads, having agreed to 'stop agean' passed the day enjoying the fun of the fair as provided by Tuby's 'dobbie-horses' – Martha's name for them. Music and singing belched forth from every pub round about; 'Farmer's Boy, Sweet Marie, Annie Laurie, or Dolly Grey', played on concertina, melodeon, mouth-piece, and tin whistle, and sung by voices over-fresh with too many 'liveners'. The recruiting sergeant, too, was always in evidence at 'stattises' and 'hirings', and many a beer-befuddled farm chap fell to the gorgeous attraction of that bright red uniform. It was a happy hunting ground for the recruiting sergeant, until the law forbade that any man should take the queen's shilling while in liquor.

Hiring fairs are about done away with nowadays, no farm servant being compelled to stay at his place a twelvemonth. But at the time of which I am writing, when a hired servant had taken his 'fastening-penny' he was bound by statute to live in and sleep on the premises from 1st December to the following 24th November; to become, in fact, the property of his master.

The hirings took place in this fashion. We would stand about in groups, either in the market or the adjoining streets, until a farmer came along. After eyeing us over like so many oxen, he would say: 'Nah, my lads, any on yer seeking a place?' Being warmed up with good ale, we answered truculently, or offhandedly at least, that we didn't 'care a damn whether we got a place or not', and, 'What sort o' chap are yer wanting?'

He would then say, 'wagoner', 'seconder', 'stable-lad', or 'cow-lad', according to which he wanted, and after singling out a man or boy that took his fancy would begin questioning him on his qualifications.

'Can ta ploo, thack, stack, and drive a binder, manage three horses abreast, and carry barley?' There was no end of questioning from both sides, for the 'fastening-penny' cut both ways, and neither man nor master could part company under a twelvemonth without some lawful excuse.

Then came the inevitable question of wage, and, as this was the only time when master and man met as equal and separate units, the man made the most use of his time. When they had agreed on this delicate point, they both entered the nearest pub, where the 'maister' treated his man to a can of ale and bound him with a 'fastening-penny'. 'Fastening-pennies' varied according to the generosity of the farmer, but a head-wagoner seldom got less than a five-shilling piece, while seconders got half a crown or so, and lads in their first year could be bound with a shilling.

The wage of a fifth-rate horseman or wagoner was from twenty-four to twenty-six pounds, though I have known cases where a good man received thirty pounds for the year. Second and third lads got from sixteen to twenty-four pounds, while the first working year of a lad's life could be bought with a five-pound note.

So that was how we carried on before the Great War. Then the Agricultural Wages Act came into force, and altered the custom of hired servants being tied for the twelvemonth. To me it always seemed a wretched business, especially for a lad of thirteen or fourteen, to be taken like a sheep or calf to market and sold to the highest bidder. No wonder if some of them ran away and took the king's shilling, rather than be tied for a whole year to a bad place.

But to get back to the 'stattis', or rather, back to Ben Cobb's covered wagon, for I'm sure you've had enough of Martlemas Fair, with its ale-drinking, singing and fighting; its merry-go-rounds and side-shows, including a new innovation called a moving-picture show. We three lads, not being fully alive to the vagaries of Ben Cobb, sought out the carrier's cart at six-thirty, because a cardboard clock at the back pointed to six-thirty, with the words 'We start at' printed over the top. No one else, however, seemed to have taken any notice of that imitation clock, for it was some time later before any of our party turned up. Then they rolled up in twos and threes, in various stages of freshness, from market merry to helplessness.

At seven-thirty old Jasper came clumping across the yard, bearing on his halter-shank the swaying form of his master. Ben was a cantankerous old chap when under the influence, and though we all offered to help in yoking up, Ben would allow no one to touch his horse, saying: 'When I can't yok' mi own 'oss I'll gie up!'

So we had to content ourselves with watching Ben fumbling about with straps and buckles which, to his bleary eyes, must have appeared double in number. But we got hitched up at last, and glad we were to hear the old roan's feet go clip-clop on the rough stone setts.

Homeward-bound, the musicians played merrier than ever, while the pleasant scents of the covered wagon gave place to the reek of tobacco and strong ale. Out in the country it was quite dark, with a ground fog bathing old Jasper's feet as he went clop-clop-clop, beating time to the jingle of his harness, and no doubt eager to reach his stable.

A candle swayed in the roof in a little red lantern, and from my seat at the back I watched it make grotesque shadows of Martha's bonnet, which was all awry, while a stray lock hanging down her forehead gave her shadow a strange resemblance to a nag's head. Her eyes were rather inflamed, too, and she seemed inclined to be fractious, all of which I put down to the smoky atmosphere. Old Ben was the most difficult problem on our homeward journey; being over far gone, he had an alarming habit of falling overboard at frequent intervals. The old horse – from force of habit – always pulled up whenever he felt the driver leave his seat, so Ben always escaped being run over. But it startled his passengers, until they became used to Ben's little ways. It caused no end of delay getting him loaded up again; for Ben was touchy when in this state, and resented any help to get him back to his seat.

Ben had two great virtues which never failed to impress a stranger when travelling in his cart. Firstly, he was merciful to his beast, and by that virtue never hurried him uphill or down, but kept a steady pace of five miles per hour. His other virtue was his implicit faith in old Jasper; he hung the reins on a hook in front of the wagon, and trusted to horse-sense.

We never seemed to mind, however, but just looked on a journey with old Ben as a pleasant adventure. And so we sang our way back along the dark long road, and I must confess the songs and stories took on a spicy tap-room flavour. Ernest Gill, bluer and redder in the face than ever, sang funny songs until the tobacco fumes overcame him and he slid down among the straw in the cart-bottom. By the time we reached the Black Lion a general drowsiness had settled over all, with just a chirp now and then, like nestlings in the eaves at bedtime. I remember feeling a bit aggrieved and put-out like, because one of the servant girls fell asleep with her head on my shoulder. I had no chivalrous instincts toward the fair sex at that age, and greatly resented the liberty. I kept saying 'Hey-up' every time the wagon lurched and bumped her head on mine, until Mrs Butterfield, seeing me give her a nudge with my elbow, threatened to 'screw my neck round if I didn't let the wench a be', and called me a 'mar-darse'.

It was uncomfortable and stuffy for us young ones squeezed in the back of the cart, and I ought to have been more generous to Doris; poor kid, she was only sixteen, and according to Elsie – who was two years older – they had been up since four o'clock that morning, having been promised a day at the 'stattis' providing they did all their morning's work before setting off.

And so we got out at the Black Lion, the older hands for a freshener, we youngsters for a breath of fresh air. It was now ten o'clock, and the Black Lion was turning out; but, as old Bob Dale said: 'What does it sinnify? We 'em all bonny-fides, an' 'titled to refreshments.'

So they got out – except for Ernest Gill, who was beyond getting out – and sang and danced to the benefit of 'Bill Munday (Proprietor)' for a solid half-hour. After that the party woke up a bit, and we sang and played, with the harness jingling, and old Jasper's rhythmic clip-clap-clop, until we drew up at the Little Brown Jug on the stroke of eleven. We were still 'bonny-fides', so had to get out for 'an odd un to see us whome', said Ben Cobb. I was dog-tired, but the thought of waiting another half-hour at the Little Brown Jug decided me, so I said to Sam (Bennett's lad): 'I'm walking the rest, it's only two miles.'

Now Sam was eighteen, same age as Elsie, and, after whispering to her a moment on the subject, they set off to walk together. I thought it a dirty trick to desert a pal like that and walk off with a girl; but Bob fra' Wood's, Doris Hind, and little Harry Butterfield came along with me, so we followed along behind the other two.

It was nearly midnight when we reached home, and I so far unbent from my ill manners as to allow the weary little Doris the support of my arm, while young Bobbie did likewise on her other side. Thus the four of us frogged it along the dark lane. We tried to sing, but didn't make much success at it, for it had been a busy day, and for lads and lassies whose normal bedtime is nine o'clock, singing at midnight takes some doing. We caught up with Sam and Elsie, who were waiting at the farm gates – and Sam was never the same lad afterwards, but ran down to the village at nights, instead of joining the sing-songs in the stable – and we stood there a minute or two listening to a horse's hoofs beating out a rhythm on the road we had just come along. A light twinkled through the trees where the lane turns down to the village, and as it came nearer we caught a sleepy, thick-voiced refrain:

Oh, it never returned, it never returned,
And its fate is still unlearned,
But from that day till this, they are weeping, watching, waiting,
For the ship that never returned.

The chorus was appropriate, for not many more times was the carrier's wagon to bring its load of Martlemas merrymakers. The railway drove him off the road, and a railway carriage doesn't lend itself to merrymaking and mirth. Even after a hundred years of railway service, people still sit stiff and glum in a railway carriage, or hide themselves under sheets of paper, whereas if the same people sat behind a horse they would become as chirpy as linnets.

Seven

A NIPPER ON THE RAILROAD

I WENT BACK TO my place at Hill-top Farm feeling full of beans after my week's holiday. Being only a month short of my fifteenth birthday, I ought to have known the wiles of the missus better. She had become quite affable some weeks before leaving-day, and, like a silly young fool, I expected the change to last. Of course, it didn't, and I became as big a drudge as ever; in fact, being now more experienced, even more odd jobs were piled on my shoulders.

But I didn't take the same pleasure in seeing to things as I had done during my first year, and, though I still took great interest in the welfare of the cattle, and still thought old Short the best horse that ever was, I often thought of my schoolmates, many of whom were now working on the new railroad, with their weekends at liberty. I should have been content where I was, however, had the missus been more agreeable, for I liked farm work, especially ploughing, and had no idea whatsoever of changing my fortune before another year was up.

It happened in this way. As I mentioned in my first year, George was apt to get market merry whenever he went teaming to town, and when in that state seemed to take a fancy to me as a sparring-partner. Well, I kept out of his way all I could, which was difficult at times, seeing that he was my bedmate; but, as he hadn't a word to say wrong to the cat when sober, and didn't get merry many times during the year, I thought I could put up with his little bits of excitement. I was pretty scared though, and used to hide

in the cart-shed until he had quietened down or was snoring off the effects
among the hay in the stable. His first bout during this year happened soon
after I got back, and had its amusing side, too. It was the Christmas Fat-
stock Fair, and George took two porkers in the heavy cart with young
Flower in the shafts. The miller had a fat heifer to take, and, as driving a
lone beast is always difficult, he brought it up to our place to go along with
three of ours; the miller giving me sixpence for relieving him of the seven-
mile walk, while he and his missus went to town by carrier.

After the market was over he must take George into The Cleaver for a
drink. Now, it isn't so bad for a wagoner to call at every pub on the road
and thus get a load on by degrees, it simply makes him a bit lively; but
George and the miller sat in the pub knocking off pints of ale heedless
of the fact that we had a spirity young mare to drive over seven miles
of slippery road. It was a fortnight before Christmas and freezing like
anything. It was six o'clock when at last – with the help of the miller's wife
– we got them to leave their ale drinking, and tumbled them both into the
bottom of the cart. It was a perilous journey for a lad to take with a high-
mettled mare, and the wonder is that I got them home with nothing worse
than a pair of bloody noses. The fun began after we left the town lights
behind and were out in the country. Our only light was a stable lantern tied
to the axle-tree – in defiance of the law against that custom – and Flower
could see a shadow bobbing in front of her forelegs. She snorted, stepping
sideways to avoid it, and, as it couldn't be avoided, she broke into a trot.
I had enough on to hold the mare on the icy road, without time to look
what was going on in the cart; but the jolt of a springless cart had a serious
effect on the ale. There was no end to the curses on my eyes if I didn't let
the mare walk; but that I couldn't do, and so the ale churned up until it
spread over the cart-bottom.

After a mile or two Flower settled down to walk, and even then it was
tricky work keeping her on her feet. The miller's wife was seated on the
front board placed across the middle of the cart, and every now and then,
as the mare made a jump, or slithered on her haunches, would exclaim:
'Oh, deary me!' 'Would to God I'd come back wi' the carrier! Niver agen,

if the Lord spares me, will I come home this-how!'

After each pious ejaculation she promised me 'a silver sixpence gin I got her home safely'.

George had taken two pigs to market in the morning and, I regret to say, I brought two drunken pigs home. They got arguing – in a friendly sort of way at first, until George started waving his arms about. Then they began pushing at each other. Now, there isn't enough space in a heavy cart for two drunken men to start scrapping, especially with a lady and a young lad in the 'ring', and I heard knuckles rapping hard on the cart sides that had been meant for softer bodies; but I kept driving on, leaving the two pigs to be separated by the miller's wife. She took George by the collar, trying to part them, and George, unable to stand up, groped for something to hold on to, which happened to be my leg; and I, feeling my feet going, clutched at the reins, pulling Flower over the grass verge, with the near-side wheel stuck in the ditch.

And that was where our outing ended. Flower lay quite still, broadside on, while I struggled to unloose her chains. She wasn't much hurt, but – like me – was all a-tremble with fright. Leaving George and the miller, who were nearly sober again, to be helped along by Mrs Miller, I hurried home. I didn't get thanked, either, for my part in the affair; the missus rated me soundly for having the best mare down, and when George arrived – in a terrible ferment – he chased me round the buildings for leaving him to walk home. Thank goodness it was easy to escape him in the dark for I was scared nearly to death, and slept that night in a 'fotherham'.

Next time I went home I found mother had got to hear of my escapade – for a cart isn't left in a ditch all night without provoking a bit of talk – and advised me to go home if ever George carried on like that again. Like the rest of the village, she now went in for lodgers – she had two joiners laying with her – and they gave their advice on the matter, saying what opportunities there were for a lad like me on the railroad.

Well, I stuck it all winter, and was quite satisfied. George was a very decent chap when he wasn't teeming, and Harry, the cowman, was a good sort at all times. My hands, too, never got in the sad state of my first winter. And so I got through the usual run of a farm lad until March, when George went teeming again.

We had no station in the village then, and everything – tillage or cattle-food – had to be fetched from town. As it happened, Tom fra' Bennett's went teeming on the same day; they had both gone for tillage for the potato and mangold fields. I saw them both returning, seated on their drays in a half-asleep attitude, and I knew if the lively Tom came home silent he must have shifted a fair amount of ale. I made myself as scarce as possible and everything went all right until after tea. Then Mr Bennett called and began rating George for treating his man to a lot of ale. George swore at him, and, ordering him to mind his own business, followed him to the yard doors to: "Ev it out like a man.'

The missus followed, trying to calm George down, for Mr Bennett was a good neighbour and she didn't wish for George to offend him. I was left in the house finishing my tea; my fear gave me courage or I never should have dared what I did; I crept upstairs, brought down my tin box, and stole silently away through the stack-yard.

Little Norwood lay in a valley, and the new railroad had to make deep cuttings into the hills on either side, 'tipping' the rock and soil into the valley, thus shutting in Little Norwood on its eastern side. It was on this seven-mile stretch of the Hull and Barnsley and South Yorkshire Railway that I intended making my fortune. That I never did make a fortune may be due to lack of enterprise on my part, or it may be that I was born to be a farm labourer. Be that as it may, I never saw or heard of a workman making his fortune thereon.

I tramped that bit of railway dozens of times before anyone took a fancy to me. The first ganger man I approached was not encouraging. He was a big burly man, wearing white moleskins, and looked like a prize-fighter. His language would have turned the stomach of a fish-porter, as he bellowed at me to 'get back to the b— turnip field'.

I left him hurriedly, like a dog that has received the boot, but he called me back, and in a shade gentler voice said he didn't need a nipper, but I yet 'might get on round one o' the steam-navvies'.

So I thanked him and went to where a steam-navvy was tearing up the earth in a huge steel bucket, swinging round, and dropping its contents into a long line of tip-wagons. I was interested in the process, especially as there were two powerful horses engaged – one to 'fly' the empty wagon under the 'navvy' and one drawing away the full ones. The ganger man, however, was full up at present, and so were they all as I tramped the sleepers for about three weeks. Then one Monday morning I came across a gang at breakfast time and was surprised to see a man wearing a black straw hat reading to the navvies out of the bible. It was the navvy-missioner or 'sky-pilot' as they called him, so I waited until he had finished before I approached the ganger. I was feeling dispirited in my search for fortune, and as the missioner continued to read I heard him finish with: 'Be strong and of good courage, afraid, neither be thou dismayed; for the Lord thy God shall be with thee, whithersoever thou goest.'

He closed his book and chatted to the men and I felt greatly helped by his words; it seemed as though they were specially meant for me that Monday morning. I walked timidly up to the ganger man – perhaps my walking timidly up was the reason for my failure to get a start – but before I could speak the missioner had clapped his hand on my shoulder, asking: 'And what country tramp are you, young man?'

He was a very pleasant-spoken fellow, and soon drew from me who I was and where I came from. More than that, he knew a lad was missing from one of the steam-navvies – he made it his job to know all these little wants of the railroad – and, taking me by the arm, introduced me to the ganger.

So I got a job at last, 'doggin'-on'; that is, hitching the horses on to the wagons by a chain hooked on to a spring-bar. Thanks be to the 'sky-pilot', I was still working a pair of horses. The pay – though I thought it a tidy bit of money then – was not on the scale out of which fortunes are made. I got threepence per hour, working from six to five with one and a half hours for meals, excepting Saturday, when work stopped at one o'clock. If we got in a full week I drew about fourteen shillings, which, of course, was very good pay. Navvies, by the way, got fourpence to fivepence an hour, while some of the more important jobs around the navvy called for sixpence.

All that summer I kept on the railroad. The navvy-missioner was a splendid chap, very good natured, as he had need to be, listening to the reviling he got from some of the navvies. He took particular interest in the young people, encouraging them to come to the mission-hut at nights for games of draughts or darts or to read books and magazines in the little reading room. But he never preached, except to the inhabitants of Tin Town on Sunday; he had too sure a knowledge of human nature to lecture at the wrong time.

In that motley crew I have heard decrepit old navvies, lost to the world in filth and rags, declaim on the beauties of Shakespeare or verses of some great poet. We don't realise nowadays what the unemployment insurance has done; for many of those vagabond tramps were men of education, whom drink or misfortune had robbed of all self-respect.

There were good men and out-and-out scamps to be found among them, but I think it was one of the latter I met on my first day going to work. I was feeling well pleased with myself as I trudged down the road with plenty of time to get there before six a.m. A bottle of tea in one pocket and my 'snap' in a red handkerchief, I went whistling merrily along, when a robin flew out of a haystack by a field gate. My bird's-nesting instinct caused me to look over the gate, as a haystack was a robin's nest. I was wondering if I had time to climb over the gate when an unseen voice said: 'Got a chaw o' bacca, matey?'

I looked at the bottom of the stack, and found the voice came from a red-eyed, sandy-haired, ferret-faced little man, who had used the lee-side of the stack as a doss-house. He was busy doing a bit of chiropody work before putting on his boots, and while attending to his feet, kept casting his little bleary eyes at me. I didn't like the look of him, and was turning to go when he repeated his question; so I told him I didn't smoke.

'Ye havna a copper on ye for a mashin' o' tay, young gentleman?' he asked, thrusting his feet into a pair of worn-out boots. I ought to have said no, and left him; but not being a good hand at snubbing, I gave him a penny, saying that was all the copper I had.

'Thank ye, young meester, thank ye!' he said, getting on his feet and hobbling to the gate. 'It's about dead-beat I am for a mashin' o' tay, and me walkin' the way fra' Thorne sin' Sunda' afternoon. Forbye,' and he gave me an evil wink, 'if ye'd another copper now for a bite o' bread and cheese – but then, if ye ain't, ye ain't, sonny.'

I had a shilling on me which I had carried about for weeks, not daring to break into it until I got a job; so, like the country lout I was, I told him I had a shilling but should need it myself. He didn't seem a bit crestfallen about that, but commended me for being such a steady young man.

'Why!' said he, 'gin I see ye alookin' o'er the gate, I says to mi'sen, Sandy, I ses, yon's a fine bonnie lad noo, a doose lad, yo, 'at dosna need to step aw the wa' fra' Glesga' to earn his livin'.'

'Have yer walked all the way fra' Glasgow?' I asked, like an innocent.

'Every step, young meester!' And coming through the gate the evil little reptile told me a tale of how he was 'ain brither to the agent o' this 'ere railroad', and, becoming very confidential, added: 'Not a word o' this to a soul, mind ye; it's just twix you an' me as owd pals. Aw' the wa' fra' Glesga' it is, jist to see my ain brither, and now belike I wonner see him.'

'Oh, you might, he comes up the line most mornings!' I answered, hoping to cheer him up, for he seemed very sad at the thought of not seeing his brother.

'Nay, laddie, for Sandy winna disgrace his brither wi' the siet o' claes the like o' this; forbye now, an' I could borrow a shillin' to make me preesentable – but theer' and the poor little chap shook his head despairingly.

What could I do but lend him my shilling, which he promised faithfully and with many words to pay back with interest when he had seen his 'brither'. I doubt if a shilling would have made Sandy presentable, and it was more than likely to further inflame his little red eyes. But anyway, as a parting shot, he saw my 'snap' wrapped up in the red handkerchief, and whiningly said: 'Ye wean't in brocht mair tommy na' ye'll require, belike?' So I gave him a slice of bread and bacon, and, promising to be on the look-out for him returning my bob, I hurried to my first day's work on the new railroad.

I found them a strange lot to work amongst. Though many of them were decent, hard-working fellows, those that weren't, weren't. They were just the off-scourings of every county in England, and I heartily wished myself behind a pair of useful plough-horses. There were four of us lads working around the steam-navvy: the youngest 'fatting' wagons, a stinking job, for which he got twopence-halfpenny per hour; another lad carried tools to the smithy; I was 'doggin'-on'; while a big, strong youth was lowering wagons or 'spragging' as it is generally called. The tool-lad and general errand-boy had to 'mash' tea, and in between meals make a bucketful of skilly (oatmeal and water) for the men; and the way some of them 'golloped' it down was a sight to see, especially if they were just off the roads and pretty well famished. I had fed pigs that drank skilly with less suction noise.

We were none of us very hard worked, and found plenty of time to lark about and get into all kinds of mischief. The tool-carrier was a terror to those poor old navvies, and some of his tricks were rather disgusting; for instance, he would sometimes drop a fat earthworm in the skilly for the sake of hearing some old navvy bellow and swear when, after stirring up the mixture to get a good thick drink, he found a worm in his mug.

Poor lad, his antics cost him his life eventually. One of his jobs was to fetch powder and fuse, along with the powder-monkey, for shot firing. At sometime or the other, when the powder-monkey wasn't looking, he managed to pinch a detonator, which he carried in his pocket for weeks. He often threatened to throw it on the fire where the men sat at snap-time, just to make them jump. Fortunately for them we persuaded him not to, for, though a detonator looked a harmless little thing, we didn't know what it might do. Then bonfire-time drew near, and the lad decided to get rid of his strange firework. He placed it in his cap and put a match to it; there was a bang, and his cap disappeared along with three fingers, and one eye blinded. It was an awful warning to us lads not to play with harmless-looking detonators; and what it would have done had it been thrown on the fire in that circle of navvies is too fearful to think about. The lad came out of hospital, but never got over the shock, and died the following spring.

But about the railroad, and how I came to tire of it after the summer was over. The cutting we were in was very deep, and, I should think, more than a mile in length, resembling nothing so much as a huge quarry of hard white limestone, littered with rails, sleepers, spraggs, broken tip-wagons and spare parts of machinery. To me it was a horrible wound slashed across the fair face of the hill, and I always took more interest in the ploughmen on either side of the line than in the wonderful machinery. The wretched existence of some of the men made my soul revolt against making railroads.

Some instances of the sordidness of it all. There was the navvy found dead in a cornfield, due to excessive alcoholism, said the coroner. He was buried by the mission, his name unknown, and not a soul to care who or what he was; nobody in those good old days troubling themselves about a navvy the more or less. Another time one of them met a terrible death on the common, where many tramps and moochers camped out during the summer. There they made a rude shelter of the tin sheets, 'brattish' cloth, and timber from the close-by railroad; anything rather than pay for a respectable 'kip' (lodging), because this would mean less beer and more work. One Saturday afternoon a party of them – full of beer – lay around a wood fire in drunken sleep. They awoke to find one of their number roasting on the burning sticks, and after long delay the poor fellow was hoisted into a spring-cart and jogged and jolted to the village surgery, while he moaned and cursed piteous to hear. He was attended to by the village doctor, and then put in the bottom of a wagonette and conveyed the seven miles to hospital.

During the winter a farmer, cutting up his haystack, came across the body of a tramp who had accidentally been buried therein during haytime. He had climbed on the stack for a doss, covered himself with hay, and, no doubt being drunk, never woke up when the hay-leading started next morning.

So they came and went in those happy-go-lucky days, when one half of the world didn't know how the other half lived; and, for my part, standing on the crossroads of life, I couldn't see any good in growing up a navvy.

Had I been fortunate enough to have got in the fitting-shops or engine-sheds, it would have been different; but it required the helping hand of a friend to reach those plums, and I had no one to say a word in the right quarter. So I stuck to the steam-navvy all summer. And a blazing hot summer it was, with stifling heat in the deep cutting, made more oppressive with the stink of blastings, tubs of wagon-fat, and lack of conveniences for the workmen. In summer, too, I had done very well, getting fourteen shillings pretty regularly each week; but, alas for my fourteen shillings when autumn came, with its rainy days. My week's wage was reduced to about five shillings.

Having no one to say which way was the best, and mother doing fairly well with lodgers, I decided that a farmer's boy was a deal better off than a nipper on the railroad. So, when Martlemas came, with no improvement in the weather, I went again to the 'stattis' and got hired.

Eight

BACK ON THE FARM

I WENT TO THE HIRINGS AT DONCASTER, determined not to bate a penny less than twelve pound for the year. But so much for the new railroad, it had so lifted the level of farm wages that a farmer who knew me by sight came up and offered me fifteen pound to be his 'horse-lad and milk a couple of cows'. So, with half a crown 'fastening-penny' to clinch the bargain, I once again brought out the old tin box.

It was a four-horse place, and well-known as one of the best living places for farm chaps in the neighbourhood. Also, it was one of the best cultivated farms in the district, and along with two more farms and about twenty cottages formed the neatest, sweetest little hamlet to be found in a day's march.

The farm was known locally as the old Moot Hall, to distinguish it from its more important neighbour, the Manor House Farm, and it was supposed to have a very ancient history. A 'Courtleet' – or some such name – was held here once a year, but I think it was only an excuse to draw round the fire in a friendly chat over a jug of ale.

It was a sheep and barley farm, with a full-time shepherd and a day-lad to help in winter, when the sheep were folded on the turnips. In those days chopping turnips for sheep was an important job, while nowadays more concentrates are used, thus making the shepherd's life less harsh.

Before saying anything about my life at Moot Hall, I would like to say that being a shepherd's lad was about the roughest job on a farm during the winter months. There might be two or three hundred sheep (fattening hogs) folded on the turnips, and the shepherd, his lad – and not forgetting the dog – spent their days from daylight to dark in the field feeding sheep and dressing turnips. Artists have drawn some pleasing pictures of the shepherd leading his flock on the grassy uplands, or gazing pensively at a setting sun, but we have no picture of the shepherd in the muddy turnip field; of him and his lad sliding about in the muddy sheep pen with skeps of sliced turnips; or the lad, bending down to clean out the troughs, receiving a gallant charge in the rear from a too-playful tup; or when snow and sleet swirls round their ears and they 'chop and throw' in defiance of foul weather. That then is a picture of the shepherd as I saw him; and though he had a shepherd hut in the picture, it could only be used as a shelter at mealtimes.

Now, about my life at Moot Hall and the little hamlet of Coldwell Green, with lilacs and laburnum in every garden. I found the place a great improvement on Hill-top; even the outside of the house looked more inviting. The front door, for instance, looked alive; the front door at Hill-top was never used, and had taken on a dead appearance through lack of the hand of friendship. Front-doors, I have noticed, are like that, and respond to touch. The well-kept garden and trim lawn were a pleasure to look upon.

The missus – the most important person on a farm in the eyes of a hired servant – was a real good sort, whose one aim in life seemed to be the hopeless one of feeding her men till they were 'stalled'. For breakfast we started with boiled bacon – the staple diet on every farm – and boiled milk. Then, with bread and butter, we passed on to apple pasties, home-made jam, or currant cake; and more, we had a nice white tablecloth instead of oil-cloth. There was no measure or stint; enormous quantities were put on the table and we cut for ourselves. Indeed, it looked as though we had been engaged for the purpose of removing victuals. Dinner-time was the same big meal, and the maid always brought the roast off their table and placed it on ours, master and men living on the same joint.

But, lest I appear a glutton, I had better pass over the food and talk about work. I found a very good master, and, with a reputation for a well-kept farm, a very particular one. I found my mate, the wagoner, even more particular, and the most methodical person I ever worked under. I thought him a bit faddy at first, but when I got used to his ways, found his methods all to the good. He was a big raw-boned chap of about thirty years, who called a spade a spade, and knocked anyone down with it who dared to say otherwise. Being strict and tidy in everything, he made us all learn his habits, and even muck-forks had to be wiped clean and hung up in their proper place. As for carts and drays, they were given their inch of room under the cart-shed, and should anyone in a hurry leave a cart an inch this way or that out of its place, Albert jumped down his throat. He was no respecter of persons, either, and the boss would sometimes walk down the yard with a hayfork, strawing the yards. Then he would go in the house to look at the paper and take it easy, leaving the fork by the yard gate. If Albert saw the fork he would go to the house door, calling: 'Is the maister in?'

The boss would leave his easy-chair to see what was amiss, and Albert would then say: 'En you left a fork anent the fold-yard gate?' The boss would smile good-naturedly at the hint, though he did not like the disturbing, and say he was sorry, and 'Just take it back with yer, Albert.'

Though I didn't see much sense in carrying the habit so far as that I found the idea a good one for always knowing where to find one's tools. He was the same with his horses. There was a good trade for town-horses in those days, and all the horse-dealers knew Albert and could recommend his horses to 'turn on a threepenny bit', as the saying went. In plain words it meant the horse had been broken in to stop at 'Whoa!' and not gradually pull up in a yard or more – which was an important point in a well-trained horse. Also, Albert never considered he had broken in a horse to shaft properly until it could turn the cart in front of the shed and back it under cover by Albert speaking only and not touching the reins. It was wonderful to watch him handling three and four-year-olds till they could do almost anything but talk.

For all he was so strict, it was seldom he 'dropped the lines across them'; he didn't believe in hitting a young horse for the sake of making it show its paces. He used to say, 'Talk or whistle all the time while following a young horse, and it will never go wrong'; which was very true, for while the horse knew you were there its ears twitched back and forth in confidence; but drive it without speaking, with only the lines pulling at its mouth, and it soon became a bundle of nerves.

I acquired a great love for horses while at this place through watching and helping Albert, for he broke-in three or four youngsters every year, the boss giving him five shillings bonus for each colt sold and half a crown for the fillies. Colts were in greater demand for town work than fillies, a good seventeen-hand colt being worth seventy or eighty guineas. Our plough-horses, too, were fine animals; perhaps a little overfed to work comfortably, but it was a habit with farm wagoners to overfeed their horses, and many cross words have passed between masters and men on the subject of corn stealing.

I spent a very pleasant year working the horses, for it was a pleasure to walk after such fine animals. My line mare was a thick-set bay called Beaut, and the mother of some half-dozen sons and daughters that eventually found their way into town-service; horses were much like human beings in that respect, the best found work in the towns. Albert drove a dark-brown mare as his line horse, a very showy animal that lived up to the name of Mettle, and with a three-year-old each in the furrow, or 'offside', we had as pretty a turn-out as anyone might wish for.

I had made some progress since the time when Short and Betsey used to up-skittle the plough and I used to cry with fright and vexation. I felt now I was really a ploughman, and with a pair of fine horses before me and a clean-cut furrow behind, drew as straight a line as any lad in the village. Ploughing may be looked upon as a lowly occupation; but to me the smell of new-turned earth, the free life and fresh air, the undefinable understanding that exists between man and horse places it far above such jobs as carrying bricks and mortar or making a roadway.

It was on this farm I first became acquainted with an 'Oliver-digger'. I had often heard farm chaps decrying them, and refusing to get hired to any farmer who owned a digger. Even Albert, who had been ten years at this place, threatened to leave come Martlemas if the gaffer 'didna throw the blarmed thing ont' scrap-heap.'

The reason for this bitterness was not so much because it was a newfangled tool, as because a digger-plough had a short mould-board with a 'wing' to break up the seam as it turns over. Now, the art of ploughing had always been to leave a well set-up seam, showing neat straight lines all across the field, and these diggers did the very opposite. They may be economical, but they spoiled the art and glory of 'chalking it out', and it was a long time before some of the ploughmen took to them.

I learned a bit, too, from the shepherd, who was a dog-fancier and rather a dab-hand at training sheep dogs. He had a collie bitch called Jess. I always felt sorry for Jess; she looked so thin and was so terribly overworked. When she wasn't shepherding, she was suckling pups, and when she wasn't suckling pups, she was teaching them the art of shepherding. Poor Jess, I'm afraid hers was a dog's life. Tom (the shepherd) broke in his young dogs by coupling them to Jess's collar and setting them off to round up the sheep. In this way the pup learned the different whistles, to lie down, get by, or round up, but poor Jess got sadly buffeted in the process. However, in the end Tom would draw a good price for the pup, and Jess would lie-in for another litter.

Sometimes a farmer sent a pup for Tom to break in, and if Jess wasn't at liberty just then he broke it in with a line. Of course, the first thing a dog must learn is the lie-down whistle, the most important point in a good dog and the hardest to learn, for unless a dog drops on the instant he is not much use among sheep. Tom would have him on a short line at first, teaching him to drop at the whistle; then gradually the line was lengthened, until in a week's time, or more, the dog was set at liberty, and, providing he remembered to drop, soon became a sheepdog.

A queer old stick was Tom – as most shepherds are – and what I best remember was the way he used to carry on when the hounds were about. We lived in a fox-hunting district, and Tom couldn't abide fox-hunting. They upset his sheep, he said, and if foxes got 'too thick on t' ground, they should be shot, not chased to death.'

I remember one incident which was typical of his dour, caustic wit. We were ploughing turnip-ground behind the sheep; Tom and his lad were dressing turnips in the sheep-pen a little farther along the field, when our horses pricked up their ears and became restive, and Tom's sheep huddled into a corner of the fold. You will know what a sight it is when the hounds come in view over the opposite hill, how the horses catch the faraway note of the horn long before the ploughman hears it, and how the splendid vision comes in view, and we loose our horses from the plough for safety and hold their heads while we watch. A thread of colour weaves through the hedge on the far away hillside, and a smear of yellow and white spreads rapidly down the hill in a chorus of yelps. Two browns and a chestnut rise gracefully at the hedge, carrying pink coats, and canter after the hounds. A grey comes over; now two browns take the hedge abreast; another grey; a black; and now over come browns, blacks, chestnuts, and roans, pink coats and black coats, like a charge of cavalry, and go helter-skelter across the hillside in the wake of the hounds. So we watched, and presently along our headland came an almost-finished fox, its little red tongue lolling sideways as it passed us by. It travelled on to the end of the headland, yards along the top of the low stone wall, and jumped into the lane. It immediately jumped back again, kept on the wall-top for a few yards and to our surprise – retraced its steps toward its pursuers. It passed us again and squatted in the ditch on the other side, while the hounds were now in full-cry at the other end of the field, not more than two hundred yards away. They galloped by, a glorious sight, the dogs with noses down and tails up, baying in deep chorus. They got into the lane and the music stopped. They tried the fields over the lane, but failed to pick up the scent. The whip rode up to Tom, asking: 'Have you seen the fox?'

Tom looked as wooden as a post, and said: 'Noa! I seed som'at nip past, but I thought it wor sally' (a hare).

Which I thought very foolish of Tom, for the whip would have given him half a crown had he told of the fox's hiding place, but Tom wouldn't miss a chance of scoring against the hunt.

He, in turn, got scored against one Saturday night in The Traveller's. They were discussing the hunt, a favourite topic, when Tom started his usual cry about 'broken hedges' and 'scaring sheep to death'.

'It's cruelty to dumb animals,' he said, 'and as foxes is varmint, they owt ta be shot, not chased to death.'

Whereupon the gamekeeper – an ardent believer in the sport – replied: 'Weel, Tom, lad, I'll tell thi what to do, seein' as huntin's cruel. Next time tha finds a flea on thi piller, shoot it; doant go chasing the poor little beggar all over t' plaice, it's cruel!'

Tom was fond of a drink of ale, too, and I remember that summer helping him and the shepherd-lad to wash sheep – the sheep-wash being all too near The Traveller's. Tom kept popping across for a 'livener', for we had a big flock to put through, and before going home he decided to give Jess a bath. Alas! both Tom and his dog got into the water, and we had quite a busy time hoisting him up the steep and slippery sides, as somehow his hands always slipped off the wet stones just when we thought him safely landed. When we did get him out he threatened to brain us for laughing at him.

This, I think, was the best place I ever lived at, though I never had a really bad place; not like some, which were truly terrible to live at. I have heard of places where the food was rationed out in the smallest quantities; where bacon was put on the table half-boiled, or rather, half-raw; where bread was like flour when cut into; and the bedding as poor in quantity as in quality. But at Coldwell Green the food was of the best, the horses were pleasant to handle, and everyone in the village happy and good-natured. Every house kept a pig or a few fowls, and a tidy bit of garden with berry-bushes along the sidewalk. The 'barm man', who came round once a week with a little pony and flat-cart, bought their surplus gooseberries at sixpence a stone. Would anyone care to gather a stone of gooseberries for sixpence nowadays? And yet these folk considered they were getting a good price for their berries.

The only important person was the gentleman farmer who farmed the Manor House. He was of the fussily important sort, and alderman and Justice of the Peace. If you wanted a favour of him, all you had to do was to pump hard on the handles at each end of his name. If you omitted the handles you drew no water from his well. He was a progressive, up-to-date sort of chap, and the first person to introduce a motor car into the village. It was quite an event, watching him turn out with his car, and all the womenfolk stood at their doors, with arms folded in their aprons, to watch the squire glide down the hill. The road descended from his entrance-gates down the village to a sharp turn at the bottom leading on to the main road. At this corner the gardener's boy was posted, to warn all traffic – there seldom was any – that Alderman—, J.P., was about to descend. At the entrance-gate stood the gardener, in green apron, keeping the road clear of children and hens – for which the place had some reputation – and presently, with a throb and a rattle, out would come the car, with the old groom pushing behind. Having got safely through the gates, the alderman would call out briskly: 'All clear, Binns?'

'Yessir, all clear!' the gardener would reply. Then would Alderman—, J.P., glide slowly but majestically down the hill, past the admiring gaze of his neighbours, with the gardener and the groom pacing behind – 'Just in case, you know!' Before venturing on the main road – which was really only another by-road – the car was stopped, and the waiting boy addressed thus: 'Anything coming from the right?'

'No, sir!'

'All clear from the left?'

'Yessir!'

And the car would proceed with caution. Had he heard the terrible predictions of his groom and gardener, or the dark forebodings of the womenfolk, I doubt not he would have gone back to the yellow-wheeled gig, and the quiet little hamlet would never have boasted of having taken the lead in mechanical transport.

The other farm was a little holding of about thirty acres, kept by a witty character named Jonathan Oaks, who spent most of his time tenting a couple of cows along the grassy lanes. He had a long, uncultivated beard, and a long thin stick for driving his cows. He wore leather leggings reaching above his knees, and as he sat in the hedge-bottoms, easy-going and good-natured, I thought him the nearest approach to Rip Van Winkle it was possible to get.

As he farmed on a small scale he was always short of tools and implements, relying on his more wealthy neighbours to lend him anything he required. In haytime we had a fork missing, and the boss said: 'Why, I lent one to old Jonathan some while ago!'

So, seeing the old chap in the lane, he asked: 'Did you bring that fork back, Jonathan?'

Jonathan shook his head and replied: 'Why, bless my soul, I clean forgot all about that fork, an' I wonnered if you had!'

On Fridays he drove ten miles into the nearest town in a ramshackle spring-cart and a horse that was sadly over at the knees. His rate of progress was woefully slow, and, though the cottagers found him useful for fetching and carrying little parcels, it was seldom they went as passengers. He was fond of telling the tale against himself, how a woman threw her basket in his cart and started walking to town. When he asked: 'Won't yer get in, missus?' she replied: 'I'm in a hurry this morning, Jonathan, but ye may as well carry my basket!'

He had a goat at one time, tethered on the grass in front of his house. The goat, however, grew tired of grass diet, and began pulling the roses off the house wall. 'But I settled 'er,' said Jonathan. 'I stopped her fra' eatin' roses; I jist fixes a muzzle on 'er, see, so eh couldna ate 'em!'

Which, of course, he never did; it was just his way of talking, and when he couldn't find a target in anyone else he just had a shot at himself.

Well, I had a very happy year in this place, nicely out of reach of pits and railways; where the women and children went gleaning after harvest, and, after threshing the corn with a thatch-peg, would take it to the mill to be ground into pig-meal.

The parish church was in a village about a mile and a half away, and I attended church fairly regular, besides going to the village on Saturday nights; there was no shop in our little 'town'. I made friends with several lads in the bigger village, there being some half-dozen farms and quite a large population, and, hearing of a three-horse place who would want a young lad as wagoner come Martlemas, I decided to leave my very good place as horse lad for the sake of becoming an inferior wagoner. Both the boss and the missus asked me to stay on, and were surprised at my wanting to leave, as most lads stayed with them until they grew too big to be lads any longer.

However, I left at Martlemas, and became a wagoner when only seventeen years old.

Nine

A JOLLY WAGONER

I STARTED WORK at Church Farm with the exalted notion I was now a full-blown wagoner – or horse man, if you prefer it that way. I had no cause for conceit, for I found the sorriest lot of horses as ever saw through a collar. It was a three-horse place and most of it grassland, and my horses were Beaut, an aged dark-brown; Daisy, a very pretty little iron-grey, not more than fifteen and a half hands, with a thick, heavy mane and nice legs, showing she had breed about her, though 'dog-poor'. These were my plough-pair, with a turnip-leading horse called Farmer, white as milk and a thick, greasy leg. These, with a twenty-year-old brown pony, made up my stable, and, having grown horse-proud through driving such fine horses the year before, I determined to alter the look of things, for I felt a bit ashamed lest I should meet Albert on the road when out teaming.

The boss was a very careful sort in the matter of weighing out horse corn, and would complain that 'them 'osses is atein' ther' 'eds off', as he doled out my measure of corn. Only Jimmy, the old pony, had any flesh on, and he was fat as butter. If there was one thing I liked in this world, it was a pair of well-fed, well-groomed horses, and I very soon got them, for the boss was a good pig-feeder, with always half a dozen porkers on hand, and these he did not stint of meal. So I raided his pig-meal shamelessly, and because I was only a seventeen-year-old lad he never suspected me. The beauty of it was both he and the missus complimented me on improving the skins of my horses. So he never knew how on threshing day I would shoot a sack of oats among the horse-chaff, or pilfer his linseed-cake, carefully locked up in the chamber for feeding bullocks.

The boss, or gaffer – we usually called a master 'the gaffer', 'boss' being a new name that came in with the navvies – the gaffer, then, was an elderly man with white bonnet-string whiskers and nose and chin that 'looked toward each other and likewise bowed'. Thin wisps of curly hair were spread here and there round his head, leaving a shiny surface on the very top, and when he was cross, which was fairly often, his curls always seemed to stand upright. He and the missus had emigrated in their younger days from up north, Wharfedale way, and had brought with them strange words belonging to that district, for there's a vast difference between the speech of South Yorkshire and the northern end of the same riding. Both I and the cow-lad had some difficulty at first to understand what he said; and, as he thought his words were correct, and we thought ours the proper names for things, why, we had lots of fun at the gaffer's expense.

He used to drive round the fields with old Jimmy in a spring-cart; he could have walked round in half the time, but that's no matter. Jack (the cow-lad) was told to put the pony's 'mobbs' on. I was leading manure out of the yard at the time, and Jack came up wondering what were 'mobbs', and what part of Jimmy they were expected to adorn. I didn't know either, but as I knew the gaffer wanted Jimmy in the cart I advised putting him in and trusting to luck. Jack did so, and we found 'mobbs' were blinkers, or the bridle, though bridle is misnamed; a bridle has no eye-caps, and is only used for riding horse-back.

Jack was not so lucky one afternoon at milking-time, when the gaffer said: 'Tak piggins int' mistall an' git agait.'

Jack stared a bit, and asked: 'What's mistall?'

'Coo-us, lad, coo-us! Does thee no onnerstan' plain spakin'?'

So Jack did his best, trying to drive the pigs into the cowshed, when he was to put a gate across to pen them in. He was having a trying time, too, until the gaffer came out to see who was making his pigs squeal. Then he stormed and raved at the poor lad, for he wouldn't have his porkers disturbed for worlds.

'Ta heel wi' sich wark! Witter barn wi' t' pigs?' he shouted. 'Thoo gaumless fooil, thoo! Canst thoo gar tha wark wi'oot lakin' wi' t' pigs?' Poor Jack got it in the neck, and all because he didn't know 'piggins' were milk-buckets, which he had been told to take into the cowshed and start milking.

The missus was a motherly old soul who referred to us as 'oor lads' – 'oor Fred' and 'oor Jack' – it had a homely sound the way she said it, and was prefixed to every animal on the farm, making lads and animals into one large family. It was 'oor Daisy' and 'oor Beauty' in the stable, and when talking of the cows, referred to them as 'oor Whitefoot', or 'oor Janet', as the case might be. She looked after us well, too, though we didn't live on the lavish scale of Moot Hall. I must say she 'wore the trousers'. Being a regular attender at chapel, she was very pleased if she could see 'oor lads' there, and I began to take an interest in the chapel again. She had very strict ideas on behaviour, and if we tried to say anything 'clever' as we sat at our meals, would pull us up with, 'Noo, ha' done! It's no becomin' i' young lads!' for she treated us like children.

In one way this place differed from the usual run of farm places, in that we got no ale for dinner, neither did we slice off our own helpings. We usually drank tea, which the missus poured out into cups – basins being the usual vessels on most farms – and hovered around us, helping us to this and that. I verily believe had we been a bit smaller she would have tucked us in bed. So I stayed at this place two years and three months; the good old lady died during my second year, and I stayed on until the gaffer retired the following February.

The land, I found, was wet and heavy, being on the clay, with ditches round the fields which were never cleaned out. Consequently the land was poor through being water-logged. Wet land, however, suited my liking for a nice fancy bit of ploughing, as the seams hold together on strong heavy soil better than on the limestone soils I had been used to. The fields, too, were small – four to nine acres – and just a nice size in which a lad could practise his hand.

It suited me, too, the way we sowed autumn wheat. First I ploughed the field in eight-yard 'lands', that is, I set a 'rig' and ploughed round it until I had worked four yards on each side. I then set my next 'rig' eight yards from the first, and kept going round that until I ploughed up to my first 'land'. In this way I left an open furrow every eight yards and a raised-up 'rig' (ridge) the same distance; this was done to drain the water away, like you often see in permanent grasslands. It looked very neat too when I had finished, and I was so proud of my first attempt at eight-yard 'lands' I thought it a shame to have to harrow it out. But I got some satisfaction out of it, for we never drilled wheat on this soil, but broadcast it on the ploughing, when it came up in the seams nine inches apart, to remain a permanent record to my hand at the plough until harvest.

Oats, too, were broadcast, only barley being put in by drill, and, as far as I could see, barley might have been left out altogether, for it never did well on this land; wheat, beans and red clover being the only crops that could thrive on the clay. Now, though I fancied myself a wagoner, I could neither 'stack, thack, nor carry barley' – the qualifications always asked of a wagoner at the 'hirings' – but I had got the notion it was more creditable to be top boy in a second-class than bottom boy in a first-class, so when it came to corn sowing a man in the village was set on to do it.

He was as tough a customer as ever saw the inside of a pint pot; a long, lanky, bent-kneed man who lived on piecework all the year round. Seth was his proper name, but he was usually known as 'Owd Dodgegraft'. All the same, he was an artist to his fingertips; at sowing, plashing hedges, ditching, stacking and thatching he had no equal. But beer and his temper had barred him from ever making a living at any one of them, for if a boss passed any comments on his work, Seth downed tools and went on the beer to the full length of his money. He was always on piecework, partly because no one would employ him by the day on account of his 'throat trouble', which often kept him off work for a whole week at a time; and it was often remarked that Seth's throat never troubled him until he had earned enough to cure it.

Another reason for his always being on piecework – or by 'tak' – was because his soul revolted at the idea of being tied down in a service cottage. He preferred to be a free agent, coming and going when he pleased, and in spite of his unkempt appearance might easily have been better off than the ordinary labourer, for there was always some farmer or other requiring his services, he being a dab hand at any job on a farm.

He was a queer customer, and would argue a week over the price for a piece of work, cursing and swearing that it wouldn't keep him in 'bacca-money'. And his first words when a gaffer sent for him to fix up about a piece of work were: 'Na see 'ere, gaffer, I'm not running my b—dy blood to watter fer no man!'

That was his favourite expression at all times and, though I don't like to repeat it, you wouldn't know old Seth properly without it. After letting off steam in that way he would fix up about a price, and then rip into his work like a madman until his 'throat' came on, or the gaffer said something to send him on the beer. He was the rummiest chap I ever worked with, but he showed me the right swing for sowing corn; and sowing corn isn't the simple job it seems, but like many other farming tricks, takes a lot of picking up.

Farming must have been a better paying job in those days than now, for we grew very few roots, letting the fallow lie idle every fourth summer, and sowing it with wheat at the 'back-end'. Of course, it gave the land a rest and produced a bumper crop of wheat the following year.

The gaffer had a married son who kept a farm, the land of which joined up to ours, and we helped each other out in busy times. The son managed his farm on much the same lines as ours, and of four lads on the two farms I was the eldest. When four lads get working together without a man to keep an eye on them, I'm afraid there's often more play than work going on, and we lads had gay times shying at tin-cans on the gatepost, bird's-nesting, or falling out among ourselves when we ought to have been weeding corn or hoeing turnips.

We were greatly amused one day when drilling barley in the seven-acre. Mr John (the son) was following the drill whilst I drove the horses, and two of the lads were harrowing, when the gaffer came riding into the field, straddle-legged across old Jimmy, with no saddle, just bare-back. He always brought us a can of hot coffee for 'drinkings' when we were in any of the home fields, and he now came riding in with a can in one hand and a basket on his rein-arm. With a wide panama – which he always wore, summer or winter – he cut such a comical figure, we lads started laughing. I suppose we were too near home for it to be worth while yoking Jimmy into the cart, so he had slipped across his back as the quickest way. Of course, it was an impertinence to laugh at the gaffer, but he was a stoutish man, and Jimmy was a small pony, consequently the gaffer's feet were nearly on the ground, so we laughed in spite of the impertinence. It didn't help to subdue our mirth when the gaffer slid carefully off Jimmy's back, still holding on to the can and basket, or when he started rating us with: 'What's ta dar, lads, what's ta dar? Gin yer mind yer wark ye'll ha' enow to do b'art gizenin' like a Martlemas goose!'

But he was a good gaffer, if he did have some quaint ways. And as we sat enjoying our 'drinkings' in the hedge-bottom, he would say: 'Oor Fred's a rare lad wi' t' drill. He drawin' a straight line, he is. Deed he's makkin' a tidy job, I warrant.'

Indeed they were pleasant days, and one thing I will say about this gaffer, he was blunt and straight-spoken. I well remember a remark he made just after harvest, which was typical of the old chap. After harvest all the farmers were wanting the threshing machine at the same time, and our gaffer was talking with two or three other farmers of when they were likely to get it.

Said one: 'Weel, I'm not greatly bothered, except I want to thresh a bit o' seed-wheat for sowin'-time.'

Another said: 'I've about rin oot of whoats (oats).'

Another wanted: 'A dais choppin' for t' 'orses.'

But our gaffer spoke for all farmers, then and now, when he said: 'I can da wi' a few whoats, an' a bit o' chop an' wheat, but what I want machine for is to git a poke o' money 'gin rent-dar, come October.'

He spoke true, for all farmers had one or two days threshing of barley ''gin rent-dar'.

This place was slightly different from my two former places in that it was in the village, while the other two had been 'out o' wa'' places, so here I saw more life and entertainment in the evenings. For all that, I spent most of my nights during my first winter in the usual way of farm lads. Most stable-bins had a fox-and-geese board carved on the lid – the effort of some horse chap's pocket-knife – and while two of us bent absorbed in the game of fox-and-geese, another would play the melodeon or perhaps a mouth-organ, and we sang choruses until nine o'clock, and so to bed. The village had been invaded by navvies some years before they encroached on Little Norwood, and now a colliery was in full blast about three miles away. The result was that this village was a fairly equal mixture of colliers, bricklayers and farm-workers, and I made friends among all three classes. It has been to my benefit, too; for whether they be colliers, brickies, or farmers, they have filled my little world with good-natured, jolly sort of people, and there have been so many of the good sorts that if I have met any sore-boned ones I don't remember it.

But with the opening out of the coalfield a difference came over the rural population; they tried to imagine themselves a grade finer in the grain than were their forefathers, and even in the stables the old songs died out, along with the old games, and the melodeons would saw away at 'Zuyder Zee', 'Come back to Bom-bom-bay' or 'Has anyone seen a German Band'. These were all very well in a way, and showed we were well up in all the latent pantomime songs, but they hadn't the meat and poetry of our old songs; so during my second winter I took to stopping in my own stable and reading. I took on a fresh interest in reading through the servant girl being a member of the village library, and her being so good as to lend me her book for an hour at night. (We weren't sweet on each other, or anything of that sort, though she was a bonny lass; I'd no eye for the girls at that time. A good stable of ''osses' and a book to read while they ate their corn was all I asked of life.)

Now, my reading had been – except for the adventure books – of the goody-goody sort, school prizes mostly, of which the only two worth remembering are *Her Benny* and *The Three Holmes*. It seems strange now, how I used to enjoy reading my sister's books. There were some popular girls' books, when we lived in the park, called 'The Elsie Series', and I must have been a sentimental little ass, for I revelled in reading of the virtuous Elsie. If ever a good girl deserved to be spanked, it was that same Elsie. Well, now I found a different world of books, with real people in them, and seated on the corn-bin, by the light of the stable lantern, I pored over Mrs Henry Wood and John Strange Winter. I still consider *The Channings* one of the best books I have ever read – and for a farm-joskin I have read a fair amount.

One amusing incident is perhaps worth telling about my thirst for knowledge. The missus would have a preacher in to tea occasionally on Sundays, and as we all 'tea'd' at the same time – for the missus made no distinction about 'oor lads' – we were often brought into the conversation. It was on an occasion when the minister was there that the talk got on to good books, and I was pointed out as a lad that was 'fond o' reading'. Thereupon the minister examined me on the extent of my reading, which didn't seem to impress him greatly, for he said in a superior sort of way: 'Ah! very good! Very good, my boy, but you should read the classics!'

Now, being a young innocent I didn't quite get him right, and asked the maid to see if the book was in the library. She, however, was as great an innocent as I, and after searching the village library, came to the conclusion that *The Classics* was a new book and had not yet appeared in the village library.

Well, I managed very nicely without *The Classics* and in those two years read most of George Eliot's works, several Dickens, Thackeray's *Vanity Fair* and Emily Brontë's *Wuthering Heights*. I have found one thing in which a plough lad scores over all other working lads. What he reads he is bound to remember, for, unlike most lads, he has no distractions; and I, having enjoyed the company of Tom and Maggie Tulliver on the corn-bin, would have them as companions at the plough all next day. In this way I gathered a host of friends who accompanied me when ploughing, harrowing, or rolling corn, and, as I say, having no distractions such as football results, horse-racing, wars and politics to drive them away, they just dug themselves in, and now I couldn't turn them out if I tried.

Well, that was the advantage of living in a village instead of one of the 'out-a-wa' places; it gave me a chance to indulge in a bit of reading. And now, having told you all about it, let's get back to our work.

In haytime we were more busy than in corn harvest, for the farm having a lot of grassland, we mowed a fair lot of hay, besides having a field of clover. I used to turn out quite early in the morning when cutting grass, as the machine cuts better while the dew is on, besides being easier for the horses before the sun gets powerful. Several mornings I reached the field as the church clock was striking five, and I know of no pleasanter occupation than to be mowing grass at that hour, when the sun is scarcely touching the dew-drops, and not a soul about; with a stray partridge calling up its chicks, and a blackie piping atop of the ash tree. Maybe a magpie will come scolding, for he thinks it an offence for these humans to come disturbing him before it is well daylight. Then, it seems, you see the earth as God made it.

There is something fascinating, almost evil, about the grass-reaper; unlike the binder that waits for the corn to die and then reaps, it cuts through life, sweeping down the slender moon-pennies and toppling them over into long lines of swathes, desecrating beds of royal purple. It chatters its way through tangles of wild vetches, and leaves behind it long lines of trembling grass, cocksfoot and white clover. By seven o'clock the sun gets higher and all the grasses shimmer in drops of crystal, and the skylark dries his dewy wings in the sun, and in the shady wood the pigeons croon a drowsy note, and all the air is full of scents and hazy mists and humming bees. Another scorching day is here. Then you look at your work, and say, 'It is enough', and go home to breakfast.

So I reaped in the early morning, and after breakfast hoed turnips, or turned the hay I had reaped the day before; and when the hay was ready, built it into neat stacks, working until nine at night, and finding days all too short because life was good.

During my second summer I broke in a dark-brown colt, feeling very pleased at the idea of having a young horse in the stable; but, alas for my hopes, the gaffer sold him at the October fair, saying: 'The best place to keep a young 'oss is in yar pocket.'

I was disappointed, for he was a fine colt and the first I had ever broken in, and all I got was the pleasure of breaking him in. It's jolly fun, pulling a young horse about – at least, I thought so then – and there's no finer picture of beauty and strength combined than a wild, unbroken colt when first he feels the lines. With all four feet planted firmly apart, his shaggy mane and tail loosely flowing, his eyes glinting wildly, and his proud neck arched as the lines draw his head between his forelegs, he makes a perfect picture. Not until his mouth is flecked with blood and foam will his stout heart give in to man. And I like to imagine, when I see a sober, hard-working old town horse, what he was like as a three-year-old, for every town horse, however staunch and patient, fought and struggled and sulked for his freedom before he became the slave of a brewer's dray or a corporation cart. Well, he's had his day, and his pride and glory are wiped out with petrol, which is a pity, for there's no living thing that has the beauty of outline and symmetry as the horse, be it shire or blood-stock. This place was not noted for fox-hunting; but, being on the clay, there were plenty of hares, and several times during the winter a pack of beagles met in the village. These dogs are much like foxhounds in shape and colour, but smaller in size, standing not more than twelve inches high at the shoulder.

One day I was in the stock-yard, cutting a truss of 'fother' during my dinner-hour, when the beagles came galloping across the paddock, and, calling to the lad and the maid to come and look, we followed them. Beagle packs are hunted on foot, for they have no speed about them, relying on their keen scent to bring down their quarry, so Jack, the maid and I, seeing they were so near and well on the scent, saw no harm in running across the next field to see if they had a kill. We had no intention of following, but somehow we did, racing pell-mell over fallows and hedges, until we found ourselves a good mile away from home. Then the hounds bore to the right by the Hunger Hills, so we took a shortcut to come up with them as they seemed to be working round towards home. We climbed the hill to find they had straightened out again by Gosling Holt, and there we were, a mile away from home after half an hour's enjoyable chase, knowing we were in for a peck of trouble when we got home again. So we were, for both the gaffer and missus gave us a good 'calling' for leaving our work to run after the beagles. But it was worth it, and we were only away an hour, which didn't amount to much in the matter of wages.

In the spring of my second year the missus began to complain of her feet, and had great difficulty in getting about. Her legs began to swell, so that she had to take things easy and lie down for an hour in the afternoon. I don't know when she first took to her bed, but somehow she just disappeared from our sight, and her married daughter came to live with us and keep house. It all just seemed to happen, and all we lads knew was the missus was 'bad abed', and always we expected seeing her up either the next day or the next.

However, we only saw her once again; on a day at the end of July, when she sent for us to go up to her room. I shall never forget the shock we got and how we stood there gaping like a couple of nitwits, unable to utter a word or ask how she was or anything. We knew the missus had dropsy and was 'filling up', but it conveyed nothing to us, and now we stood staring awkwardly at a little frail face on the pillow and the great hill of bedclothes that was her body. So she helped us out with a wan smile, saying: 'Aye, lads, ye ma'well stare, for I look in a rare pickle, I warrant!'

And as we still remained tongue-tied, added: 'Thank God, it'll soon be over!'

Then, after asking us what sort of harvest we expected and inquiring of 'oor Daisy' and the rest of the horses and cattle, which we answered in short, churlish words, she said: 'Ye may be going now, lads; and God bless ye both!'

That was the last we saw of the missus, for she went a few days after, and for long after that I regretted my country manners that held me tongue-tied when I might have said a word in season.

I stayed on with the gaffer until the sale in the following February, for the death of his wife seemed to knock the wind out of his sails and he retired from farming. What else happened this year affected me greatly, and is, I think, worthy of another chapter.

Ten

THE MATING INSTINCT

THE BOY who came to live in during my second year at Church Farm was a native of the village, and, as showing how things had progressed since the opening of the pits, his wage was eight pounds in place of the customary 'fi'-pun note'. My wage was eighteen pounds when I was eighteen years old. This lad was also a choirboy, though he now only went to evening service, and through listening to his chatter on church music – cantatas and that sort of thing – I became interested, and decided to go next time they had an anthem.

I used to go to church or chapel occasionally, being persuaded to the latter by the missus, while attendance at church on Good Friday was compulsory for all hired servants on most farms in those days. I must admit, though, my religious exercises were in polishing horse-brasses, and my gods – horses. However, I became pally with a young chap who worked on 'the buildings', and on Easter Sunday persuaded him to go with me to church, our lad having informed me they were singing *The Heavens are Telling* and I ought not to miss it. I was glad I went, for Easter Sunday became a special day with me ever after. The church was packed, and as we hadn't any prayer book, and the verger evidently thought it wasn't worth his while to bring us one, we could only join in those parts we knew by heart. I found myself sitting close up to a girl with brown curls showing underneath a little furry hat, and she, seeing I had no book, invited me to look over with her. I didn't take much notice of her at first, for I was always shy and awkward with girls, and all I saw was a very small pinky-white thumb holding one corner of a very small prayer book and on the other corner was a big brown thumb, and I began to wish that big thumb wasn't so big and brown. Next thing I noticed was the smell of violets – or it may have been lavender – and it came from her. We joined in an Easter hymn, and I stopped singing to listen, for, I thought, surely no mere mortal girl has a voice as sweet as that, and dared no more open my lips to sing all evening.

I gathered up courage to glance sideways when I should have been praying for the royal family, and saw some brown curls peeping under a brown furry hat with a sort of pearl buckle at the side. I looked again instead of praying for our bishops, priests and deacons and saw the back of a navy-blue costume with a white collar, and felt somehow I was not the same lad who had entered the church, and never again would be. The pew was packed, and while the choir sang the anthem *The Heavens are Telling*, we sat wedged close together so that I felt her breathing, while her blue costume touched my coat, sending a fire through my being, so that, what with the choir singing and the scent of violets – or maybe, lavender – I was transported into the seventh heaven; I, whose only love was a well-matched team and a nine-inch furrow.

When we got outside my pal remarked: 'Who were them two wenches sitting in our pew?'

I replied that I hadn't seen any, but just then two girls passed us by, and my pal said: 'That's 'em! Let's see where they go!'

I didn't need much persuading, though running after girls had never been much in my line. The two of them stopped outside the doctor's gate. We walked past, my pal saying, 'Good evening!' and went to the end of the street. We turned again, my pal prompting me to 'say sommat' as we passed, and as we drew level I managed to blurt out: 'Hey-up!' It was the only greeting I knew, and caused a titter from the two girls, but we hadn't gone far when one of them gave a bit of a whistle.

'Let's go back again!' suggested my pal, who knew the whole business of 'clicking' from A to Z, and warned me not to say 'Hey-up!' if I wanted to 'click'. I didn't want to, but I did want to hear the voice of that angel who smelt so sweetly of violets, so I turned back, and this time my pal took the situation in hand by clearing his throat with a 'Hem!' as we drew level. This, I found, was the preliminary to 'clicking', and was answered by one of the girls saying 'Hem!' too.

And so we 'clicked'; at least, my pal and one of the girls did. The other one, with brown curls and soft grey eyes, looked on and smiled at their backchat. I just stood and stared, not daring to open my mouth lest the girl should know me for a farmer-joskin and despise me. They soon went indoors, but not before the one with the angel voice – who smelt of violets – turned to me and asked: 'Do you often go to church?' For once in my life I saved my soul and lied: 'Every Sunday.'

After that I became a regular worshipper at church, and severed my friendship with the young bricky because he referred to one particular damsel as a tart. I got smitten pretty badly, and went to church four Sundays hard-running, but the place was never packed like on Easter Sunday and I could see no excuse for planking myself in the same pew as the girl with the brown curls. She smiled and nodded to me once in the church porch, but as she never spoke I came to the conclusion I was making an ass of myself; that a bonny girl like her wouldn't be likely to talk to a farm servant, and so the next Sunday I stayed away from church.

On Monday morning I was carting manure into Sadler's acre – a little three-cornered piece we were putting in with mangolds – when who should I see coming down the road but her, a-wheeling the doctor's children out in the pram. I felt thoroughly ashamed of having to pass her in a muck-cart, and, to make matters worse, I had old Farmer in the shafts. Had I a decent horse it wouldn't have looked quite so bad, but to meet her with an old grey horse and a stinking muck-cart, I felt, would put an end to my fancy dreams, and never again would she smile at me in the church porch. However, I jerked my scarf straight, pushed my cap a bit farther back, and stared over the hedge on the opposite side of the road with a desperate hope that she might pass without recognizing who I was. But I was doomed to be caught, and just when I began to think I was saved a pleasant voice called: 'Good morning!'

'Mornin'!' I replied, trying to look surprised.

'I didn't see you at church last night,' she said, stopping the pram and smiling up at me.

There was nothing I could do after that but stop the horse, and stammer: 'No – noa – ! I – I didn't go!'

'I wondered if you was poorly,' she said, wheeling the pram to and fro with her back to the handle.

I could only stare and colour up at anyone wondering if I were poorly.

So she continued: 'I shan't be there next Sunday.'

'Oh!' I answered.

'No, it's my afternoon out!'

'Oh-aye!'

'I always go home when it's my afternoon off!'

'Oh-aye!'

And so we stared innocent-like at each other for a moment; she with her pleasant grey eyes taking in my cart, the old horse, and me stood up in the cart-body; while I could see nothing but her winsome smile shooting straight at me. And so, having stared our fill, she bent her head and said: 'I cycle home.'

''Ev yer got a bicycle?' I asked, thinking it time I said something.

'Yes!' she answered, with a little laugh. 'Have you?'

'Yis – but I don't often ride it.'

'It's a long ride from Larbrook, isn't it?'

'Aye! it is an' all. Dy yer come fra' Larbrook?'

'Yes. I generally leave our house about eight o'clock, then it gives me nice time to get in by nine.'

'Aye! That's giving you good time, it's only half an hour's ride.'

'Oh! you men ride so fast!' Then, straightening the pram covers, she continued: 'Well, I must be going, but I'm glad I've seen you!' And, looking up with a bewitching smile, 'Well, goodbye! I don't suppose I shall see you next Sunday?' And went her way.

I said 'Gee-up' to the old horse and drove on, feeling fine at having had a word with the pretty nurse maid, and thought about it all day until the idea entered my thick head that I ought to 'do a bit o' cycling come Sunday.'

After that I made some progress, and fell to wearing stiff collars on Sundays, to the imminent danger of throttling. I attended church regularly, except once a month when I waited at the Four-Lane-Ends for a fair cyclist coming from Larbrook; and though I still took great pride in my horses, my love for them was now divided and shared with something even more divine than a horse.

Then came the annual Horse and Foal Show, and I showed the colt in the three-year-olds-and-upwards class, being satisfied to get third place, for there were some lovely animals in the ring, and mine – I called him Short after my first old horse at Hill-top – was a bare sixteen hands at the shoulder.

The Show still flourishes, but the big, massive, hairy-limbed shires have gone, and nowadays the handsome shire is little heavier than a good Clydesdale. Well, it's the day of little joints and small cuts, and the Great War took the flower of horsekind along with man. The groom, too, has disappeared, and you no longer see the dapper little man in loud checks, chewing an everlasting bit of straw, and shouting himself hoarse to encourage Lady Dainty to step out. The crowds were jollier, and screw-stoppers stared out of bulging pockets, while their owners clapped, cheered themselves hoarse, and took great helpings of snuff for the purpose of raising the desired thirst.

But it was night, down in the fairground, that mattered most to me that August Bank Holiday in the year 1909. Helen had promised to meet me there, and Helen was my girl. I was allowed out until ten o'clock, being fair-night, and this year the house was filled with company; sons and daughters came to see their mother, who was now in a poor way. But sickness and death didn't trouble me at all, and I threw at Aunt Sallies until my arm ached and Helen's breast would hold no more of brooches or neckbands. We rode the same horse on the merry-go-round until it might appear we owned it through having sat so long; and we shot into the air in the swings, with Helen's curls blowing into my face, until I became drunk with the joy of life, and hoped never to be sober again. Aye! but it was great, walking round the fair with Helen hanging on my arm; and I, pushing around the stalls to get her a fair ring as though my pockets were lined with silver; and she, knowing they weren't, refusing sixpenny brooches as being extravagant, and refusing any more rides on the roundabouts unless she paid.

And so about nine-thirty we had seen enough of the fair, and, Helen having to be in by ten, we wandered off, with the steam-organ blaring. It was five minutes' walk to the doctor's house, so we turned in the opposite direction to kill time and went over the churchyard steps along the footpath. Several more couples, likewise tired of the whirl of the fairground, had come this way to cool down, but I took little heed of them, for never before had I walked arm-in-arm with Helen – until now I had been happy to wheel her cycle up the hills – and I had two or three things to say that couldn't be shouted on the busy fairground. I told her what I thought about her, while the merry-go-rounds filled the night with a lively tune and a glare of light played round the old church tower. The big white night-moths flitted over the hedge, and a few late dog-roses clung on to fading summer in flakes of greyness on the darker hedge.

I kissed her! Aye! by gum! and me never having done anything in that line since I first trotted away with my little tin box.

Well, there's nothing unusual in a farm servant staying out all night on fair-night; so after seeing Helen home I sat on the orchard fence and thought a bit. It seemed a waste of the summer's night to lie a-bed, so there I sat, long after the lights were put out in the fairground, dreaming dreams and seeing visions, where a lass with curly brown hair and grey eyes helped me to milk cows and feed little pigs on a nice little farm of our very own, and I went to plough with a pair of young horses that couldn't be matched anywhere. But, well a day, it remained only a vision, and all that remains now of that glorious night under the stars is a bit of scribble written in an old diary, for, as you know, I had always a weakness for keeping a diary and scribbling verses.

Lines written in the Orchard
Here, all around, the breath of drying summer
Perfumes the air with Nature's graciousness;
Hay pressed within the stack, and corn half-ripe.

And orchard boughs, dropping their earlier fruits.
Now from the garden-walk comes whispers
Of purpling Lavender, and fading Mignonette,
And gleaming in the dark, the silver coins
Of Honesty shine out of beds of Rue
And Rosemary, alternate, like the path of life.
In rhythmic motion, like the pulse of night.
The sleep-eyed cattle chew, and gulp, and cud;
Swallow and chew again, and grunt content.
And a Blackie sings on the midnight air
Because his Love is fair to see.

By that you will see I had got it pretty bad, though it doesn't take much
to make me break into poetry. I was sorry afterwards that I stayed out
all night, because the people in the house had sat up waiting for me, the
missus saying: 'He's only young once. Let him ha' his fling, and do na' lock
the door on him.'

I never saw the missus again, for she was buried the following Sunday
afternoon. But as for sleeping out, it was a common occurrence with many
farm servants, and was not to be wondered at when the key was turned
promptly at nine o'clock. And from experience I can recommend 'long-
feathers' (straw or hay) in a 'fotherham' as making a comfortable couch.

I began to think about pit work or on 'the buildings' as a means of
gaining that fortune necessary to set me up as a farmer at some distant
future, and decided to chuck farm service after the gaffer retired. I may
have missed the flood that leads on to fortune, but I think fate, too, had a
hand in it.

However, that comes later. For the present I was enjoying my work at
Church Farm, and – at night – hanging around the doctor's surgery like a
sick monkey with the toothache.

During the winter my world got broadened by several visits to a theatre.
I had never been inside a theatre, having been brought up to regard them
as very evil places, and when, in the larger villages, the travelling theatre
did come I noticed people were generally rather diffident about admitting
having patronised them.

So I thought, as I had been taught, they were no cop, and was a bit surprised when the doctor's two maids were treated to a performance one Saturday night. Of course, the bricky and I went, as followers, and I felt delightfully wicked at trampling on all my conventions, while I thought somehow they couldn't be so bad if she was allowed to go.

It was a long, wooden building, starting from the front ninepenny's to the sixpenny's across the centre and on to the threepenny's at the back, the seats rising step by step all the way. A woman with braided hair, long earrings, and wearing a many-coloured shawl sat in the pay-box and took our sixpences – we favoured the sixpenny's as being less swanky than the ninepenny's and, at the same time, well away from the roughs in the threepenny's.

It was jolly, groping in the dark up those wooden steps, bumping into row-ends, and choosing a suitable row out of about half a dozen in which to lead two lassies who didn't care a hoot where they sat so long as they saw the play. From where we sat I saw a row of little lamps in front of the stage, and the bricky told us these were footlights. I didn't much want his company at first, but now I was glad of it, for – besides knowing the whole art of clicking – I found he knew all about theatres; in fact, he was what we call a 'bird', so I listened, sitting close up to Helen, while he aired his knowledge of the artists.

A piano was plop-plopping something that sounded like rainwater dropping in a tub. It wasn't any of the songs I knew, but the bricky said it was fine, so I said it was fine, too. Then he said, 'You know that piece, don't you?' when the piano changed to another tune. I had to admit I hadn't quite got it, so he told us all: 'That's an extract of Beet-oven! I thought everybody knew that!'

We were greatly impressed; but were glad when the curtains were mysteriously drawn aside without anyone touching them – and I saw for the first time, the stage – and our friend was silenced.

That first experience was indeed wonderful, and, like the first kiss, or the first primrose, can never be repeated. I don't remember the name of the play – probably I never knew it – but I do remember sitting entranced and spellbound over the fate and fortune of the hero, a man named Bill Brierly, who had been wrongfully accused of some crime. How real it all seemed, and how wonderful; the scenery, the actions of the hero, and the spiteful cunning of the detective who hounded him down.

It occupied my thoughts for many a day afterwards, ploughing or harrowing, and for the life of me I could see not evil, but good, in the theatre. I suppose these old travelling-theatre plays will be considered rubbish nowadays, but in my mind they were good, wholesome fare, without any of this everlasting sex problem stuck in them. I have seen several modern plays in up-to-date theatres without getting half the enjoyment. Amongst other plays at these travelling theatres, I well remember *The Rosary*, *The Corsican Brothers*, *Lady Audley's Secret*, *Sweeney Todd*, *Maria Martin*, *Svengali* and *Charley's Aunt*. The wonderful part about them was, they put on a fresh play every night and never seemed to have to fall back on a used play to make up their bill. You cannot recapture newness, nor innocence, and though I have seen many great actors since, they never appear so wonderful as that troupe of artists who first captivated my imagination.

But, to return to the bricky and my best girl; we often visited the theatre after that first night, and from the bricky I learned to refer to the theatre as 'The Gaff!' or, more derisively, as 'The Blood Tub!' He was a regular man-about-town, that bricky. And so, though we couldn't often take the doctor's maids along with us, I became a regular visitor to the theatre. One night they played *Macbeth* and that was my first introduction to Shakespeare, for at neither of my schools had I been taught any Shakespeare, and all I knew of him was that he was a writer of plays and catchy phrases. It was not until the next Martlemas Fair that I found a row of little Shakespeare's in a bookseller's at Doncaster, and, as they were only one and four or one and six each – I forget now which it was – I bought two copies, *Macbeth* and *The Tempest*.

But I must get back to our ''osses', for we've stayed too long in the theatre, and my story is a story of ''osses and farm chaps', and ought not to take in highfalutin subjects. Well, the gaffer seemed pretty crumpled up after he lost his missus, for, without a doubt, she was the leading light of the farm. He would sit in his chair at night – and a good deal in the daytime, too – silent and musing, with his fingers drumming on the chair-arms, and all the life knocked out of him. I could have wished for him to rouse up and give us a good slating. But he never troubled us much, and left the management to his son, while we lads, knowing our work, did the best we could for him.

So the sale-day came. It was the latter end of February, and my first experience of a farm-sale. The land tenure ceased on 14th February (Old Candlemas Day), when all fallows must have been ploughed, hedges brushed and left in tenantable repair, ditches cleaned, and all gates mended and properly swung. The curious thing about the farm tenancy was, while the land was given up in February, the tenancy of the house and buildings did not expire until May. This could be made very inconvenient for the incoming tenant, and often was, for farmers – like other businessmen – can be very grudging to each other in valuation matters. However, our gaffer got out as soon as he conveniently could and went to live with a married daughter. We had a busy time the week before the sale, setting out the farm implements in the croft. Ploughs, harrows, drags, carts, all set out in rows; turnip-choppers, cake-breakers, and all the implements for land or buildings. We thought it great fun, and yet, when sale-day came, a note of sadness crept over everything.

You see, a farm-sale is not like any other business, with just inanimate objects to dispose of. It means the dispersal of one large family, all prefixed with the friendly 'oor', and how that one word ties them to you only a farmer and his men can know. 'Oor Beauty' and 'oor Daisy', whose skins now shone with good living and constant fettling with the dandy-brush, who had been my constant companions and workmates for the past two years. I trotted them in turn round the ring – one fetched twenty pounds and the other thirty-five guineas – and watched them being led up the street in all the glory of 'caddis' and plaited straw, and knew they were 'oors' no more. Little Jimmy, the pony, escaped the fate of being sold and went into retirement with his master.

And the cows, what did they think about it all? The bustle and unquiet of sale morning? They, who had stood patiently, tied up all winter, undisturbed and peaceful on their straw bed; what are they thinking of this unusual turmoil, as they stand and stare with large, frightened eyes, while strange men look in their mouths, pinch their hides, and draw squirts of milk from their udders? Goodbye! Whitefoot, Bluebell, Janet, Cowslip, and Strawberry, you are no longer 'oors'; today you are so many pieces of merchandise to be thumped, pinched, and prodded by these prospective buyers, and tomorrow you will be scattered over the countryside, strangers in strange pastures.

I suppose it's sentimental to worry over the fate of a few farm animals, but when you've fed them all winter they become as one with you, and it's no degradation to be brother to the ox, for no man or beast can live without the support of the other. And so, at night, after the buyers have gone home, and the buildings are as empty shells, with no rattle of chains or lowings from the cattle, and no Daisy to turn her eye sideways as you enter the stable, and the yards are trampled with muddy straw and discarded lunch-paper, then comes a feeling of awful desolation, and not so much as the corn-bin left to sit on, nor a fork, nor a shovel to say that someone lives here.

Well, I stayed the week out, tidying things up, and then went home for my week's holiday which I had given up at Martlemas to oblige the gaffer. He gave me half a sovereign over and above my wage, which I thought very generous of him. And so we parted, having got on very pleasantly with each other for two years and three months.

Eleven

THE FARM IN THE WOODS

I WENT HOME with the intention of giving it all up. I had a great notion of getting work at the new pit that was being sunk at Little Norwood, for I was now nineteen, and it seemed a great age, and if I was to make a fortune and win Helen I had better get where I could addle some brass.

I said nothing at home about having got a 'gal', and mother thought I was seeking work at the pit for the pleasure of living at home. That certainly was a great inducement, but I had come to like farm service so much that nothing but Helen could draw me away from it.

So after my week's rest I tried for a job at the colliery; but as I was not a sinker, nor a fitter, the engine-wright could promise me nothing for several weeks, as labourers seeking work were as plentiful as blackberries. Then one day a farmer called to see me, having heard I was out of work. He farmed an eight-horse place close by where we used to live in the park. It was a lonely place, surrounded by woods, the farmhouse and buildings being entirely hid amongst the trees. His second horseman had run away, sacrificing his pay rather than remain buried alive in the woods. However, it suited me to revisit the haunts of my childhood, so I decided to become engaged until the following Martlemas.

It wasn't only the loneliness that had frightened away my predecessor. The farm was near to a large lake that ran up to the Hall, and was the haunt of waterhens, coots, and wild ducks, and the noise they made in the dead of night was unbelievable unless you heard them. Beside the waterfowl, there were owls and sparrowhawks calling out all night, while occasionally a fox would be heard making its double 'ow-ow' in the woods and meadows. I had always thought that Nature slept during the night-time, but not so there, for the air was filled with the most weird noises I ever heard.

Added to this, there was a private road through the wood leading to the farm. It was about a mile long, and it cut off a considerable distance when coming from town. This was an advantage in summer, when the nights were light, but in the dark became almost an adventure. The wood was overrun with rabbits, and when cycling along in the dark they would pop out in front of the cycle, and, if you weren't thrown off, the rabbit skedaddled along in the glare of the acetylene light. It was amusing, but annoying, for you couldn't speed up on that last mile for fear of coming a cropper.

Another cause – so I learned from my predecessor – was George, the first-wagoner. He was a big, fair-haired lad of twenty-two, with a chest like a dray-horse and arms like shoulders of mutton. His great obsessions in life were ale and ''osses'; anything other he looked on as weak and effeminate. When he drank he was a fool; and when sober, a bully.

There were three of us living in: George, myself and the stable-lad. George and I had four horses each to look after, while the lad helped among-hand and saw to the galloway (pony), and a day-labourer drove one pair of my horses. The living was no better than it might be, and lacked the motherliness of Church Farm or Moot Hall. Of course, it was a busy job cooking for three hungry lads, but the bacon never got enough boil, the milk was skimmed, and the ale watery.

We were allowed out until ten o'clock Saturday and Sunday nights, and as the nearest town or village was three miles away we generally slept in the stable on Saturday nights. Often in the early hours of Sunday morning we rolled out of our straw and went birds'-nesting or rabbiting, and sometimes we went fishing with improvised lines in the lake. These, of course, were private waters, but one is allowed to do almost anything at daybreak on Sunday morning. We spoiled our sport when we took the boss's gun to catch rabbits. We had often thought what fun it would be if we could smuggle the gin out of the house some Saturday and slaughter a few rabbits while the keeper slept. It made too much noise, however, and we didn't go out many mornings before a keeper met us, took our gin off us, and carried it to the boss. Then there was a fine old row on, for he was a mightily important sort, who thought himself no end of a fellow; so that put a stop to our shooting.

I remember one Saturday night the lad and I got home by ten, for it was a cold, wet night, and we didn't fancy sleeping out. George, of course, never left the pub until turning-out time, and the door was locked at ten. Well, we slipped off our boots and stole silently into the kitchen, and there was the gaffer, snoring peacefully in his chair with his mouth wide open. In that posture he had lost all his pomposity, while a glass half-full of whisky and a wedge of cake on the table seemed to denote he had done himself well at market. Jack (the lad) was a daring young nipper, and, seeing the cake and whisky waiting, gulped the whisky down – and it was whisky in those days – and stole quickly upstairs with the cake. We didn't get treated to much sweet stuff at this place, so Jack and I enjoyed the cake before getting into bed. We hadn't long got settled down before we heard a commotion down below. It was George returned – slightly soaked – and, seeing a light in the kitchen, had come blundering in, waking the gaffer with his noise, while the commotion we heard was caused by the gaffer finding his whisky and cake gone and George there. They were both too muddle-headed to search out the real culprit, and were going at it hammer and tongs. Then the mistress came on the scene, and settled the pair of them. Of course, we were fast asleep when George came upstairs.

George, like the gaffer, was one of those thickheaded sort of people who never see anything until it knocks them down. As I said, we had four pairs of horses, good ones too, and as the fields were large ones of twenty to thirty acres we had a chance to match our skill against each other. I believe I was as good as ploughman as George, if not better, and he didn't seem to like it. But the trouble came over our horses, and though I resorted to underhand methods, I got my own way in the end. George's line-mare was a high-mettled dark-brown, very fine skinned, that couldn't stand the lines over much without rearing on her hind legs. The way he abused that mare was shameful, reining her up and using a curb bit to steady her down, while his thick head couldn't see that the tighter he reined her in the more irritable she became. When he could do nothing with her he decided to swap her for my line horse, a quiet, sensible young horse, named Captain. Being head of the stable he had the right to pick his team. So I changed over with him, and after driving Violet in a smooth bit and loose rein for about a week got her going fairly steady, though she was very temperamental and would prance about if spoken to a bit sharply.

Then George wanted to swap back again, for the mare was, no doubt, the best-looking thing in the stable; and then the trouble began. I refused to give her up, so we got shoving and pushing one morning – we bridled out at six a.m. – and from pushing we got to scrapping at that early hour. I was no match for George at scrapping, and got knocked about pretty well on the stable floor before I decided to give in.

Well, I didn't intend letting him get away with it so easily as that, so I resorted to a reprehensible practice that was fairly common in the show-ring in those days. I gingered her up. Perhaps nowadays many people who hear the expression to 'ginger up' have no idea what it means. It was the practice in the show-ring, if a horse was slow in his paces, to chew a piece of ginger-root and give the horse an injection. This irritated the animal, making it pick up its hind legs and step out as though it were full of beans. It was an evil practice, and I was sorry to do it. But next night I went to the druggist for some ginger-root, and the next morning I knew I should have the mare back again. The poor animal kicked and reared, side-stepped and plunged until man and horse both were beside themselves with temper, and the boss coming in the field and seeing the antics of George, threatened him with the police-court if ever he took the mare out again. Poor George, thickheaded and conceited, the veriest child might have guessed I had interfered, and all he said was: 'The mare's no dam' good, an' tha can hav' 'er.'

Only Walter (the day-man) saw through it, and he congratulated me.

Though it was a lonesome spot in winter, when the long winding lane was impassable in snowdrifts and the tall trees were capped in snow and the farmstead seemed to be buried in a Canadian forest, so that we were cut off from the outside world, it was delightful when the summer came, especially in June, when the beech trees were decked in their loveliest shade of green. I hadn't much time for exploring the woods, however, for the boss was pretty keen and liked a full day's work out of his men and horses. We yoked-out at six a.m., which meant getting up at four-thirty, and were not supposed to reach the stable until six at night, Saturday included; so, having to be in bed by nine didn't give us much leisure. Mostly we played tip-cat in the grass-field, or – if the keepers weren't about – went fishing in the lake or rabbiting along the wood-side.

One night we had an interesting entertainment, watching the keepers digging out an earth of fox-cubs. Three keepers had been digging all afternoon, and not until night did they reach the cubs. The earth was in a disused rabbit warren, and the passages and side-runs leading to the den seemed without end, while tree roots had made the digging slow work.

It was a wonderful piece of work, showing how diligent had been the vixen in preparing her home, for the dog-fox never shares in any domestic responsibilities. They – the keepers – had dug along one passage, to find it led to the larder, where a freshly killed rabbit, a partridge and an old broody hen of ours that had been sitting in the cart-shed lay buried under loose soil. They were all fresh, with scarcely a maul-mark on them. In another direction they came across bones and refuse, while many of the passages were just bolt-holes, or, if you like, emergency exits.

We were fortunate to be there and to see them get down to two little balls of fur half-buried in loose earth. Not until the keeper pointed them out did we see them, for they were the same colour as the soil, and crouched, all curled up, to escape the eye of any marauder. Then came the delicate task of picking them up, which one keeper did while the other held open a sack, and a bit of sharp work it had to be, for the little ball of fur became a little fury when touched, and had the keeper not taken it up well by the scruff his fingers would have suffered.

They were two pretty little things, with sharp, bright eyes and pointed ears and sharp noses, and lay quite still unless a hand touched them, when their little jaws and white, baby teeth snapped together like rat-traps. The keeper tied a long piece of whipcord round the neck of one cub, and though its teeth snapped together in fury all the time he handled it, when he put it on the ground it just froze and lay as though dead. It was remarkable, for, as soon as ever a hand touched it, it tried to run off, its little teeth working like a row of needles.

I see nothing cruel in fox hunting, but it seemed a shame to be taking those cubs away from the mother and transporting them to some district where the hunt was getting short of foxes, for that was the sole idea of digging them out – just that they might be hunted to death some otherwhere. There were three cubs altogether, for we had often watched the old vixen playing with them in the dusk along the wood-side; and we had to freeze to watch them, for at the least movement on our part the fox and cubs would vanish as though the earth had swallowed them up. Where the vixen was, and the other cub, while all the digging was going on we never knew, but we never saw them again, so no doubt they were hid in one of the many passages, and when night came they moved out to fresh lodgings.

It was amongst these woodland scenes we spent our evening leisure, for the villages were all too far away, excepting Saturday, when we got an hour's extension. The only event of interest in the village, so far as I remember, was once when a marionette show was there. I found the dolls very amusing, but nothing compared to the travelling theatre, so I will not weary you with a description. My most important night was Sunday night, when I cycled six miles to meet Helen.

Her father was the coachman at one of the big houses, and being a coachman meant he was a man of some standing, while I was but a farmer's boy. Consequently he never heard of my existence while I lived at Church Farm, for we both knew that we were too young to start sweet-hearting, and as her father had strict ideas of propriety we thought it wisest to say nothing until we became grown up. So this year – I being nineteen and Helen eighteen – we decided to be open and frank about it, and the news was broken. First to her mother, who approved, subject to my being a decent lad. Then her dad was let into the know. He commanded that I be brought into his presence and examined, for he would 'have none of this back-sliding business, but mun show his face like a man.'

I suppose it's a trying time for every man, being introduced for the first time into 'her family', but to me it was very much so, for the distance between a coachman and a farm lad was – in those days – terrific. So I tried my luck one Sunday afternoon in May, when the horses were turned out to grass and I was at liberty to take tea with Helen. I found them a homely couple and quite worthy to be the parents of so fine a girl as Helen; but, though they both made me welcome, I was shy and awkward, and my answers were not of the kind to impress anyone into a favourable opinion. After examining my outward points – like the true coachman he was – my pedigree had to be sought after, lest I be dismissed as a poor hack. It was searched for in this manner.

'Are you aught a-kin to John Kitchen, the gardener at Little Norwood Hall?'

I confessed I was not, so, with another glance at my outward form, he continued: 'Oh! I thought you might be – coming from there.'

Then my future mother-in-law helped with: 'There used to be some Kitchens over Stancey way. Perhaps you know them?'

Again I shook my head, and answered: 'No, I don't know anybody that way on.'

I was given another chance by the dad saying: 'There used to be a butler by the name of Kitchen when I lived at Sherwood Hall. Something after your make, too, he was!' and he looked hopefully at me, thinking this time he had surely found my pedigree.

But no, my pedigree could not be traced to any of these worthy gentlemen, though I was willing to claim descent from any or all of such true blood if only it won favour in the eyes of Helen's father. But to admit I was the son of a cowman – and half an orphan to boot – was more than I dare risk. So while Helen smiled encouragement from her seat on the low windowsill, I said to the geraniums and fuchsias that flowered over her head that my father came out of Lincolnshire, which was quite true, and that he had been in gentlemen's service, which was almost true, as he was cowman on a gentleman's estate. So my pedigree was worked out satisfactorily, and we drew up for tea. Helen – whose home name, I found, was Nellie – poured out the tea and her mother buttered muffins, hot from the hearth.

I nearly fell at the next fence, when, over our tea, her father asked: 'What's yer fancy, then, for the Derby?'

It was an awkward question, for I have never taken a keen interest in racing, and I didn't then know the name of a single horse entered in the race, while, of course, a coachman knew every winner months before the event.

So I looked helplessly across at Helen, and saw she was making signs with her mouth which seemed to make 'My Nora', and I ventured to say 'My Nora', and hoped for the best.

'Nay, man, I meant for this year – what's your fancy for this year – though I'm glad to hear you spotted the winner last Derby.' Without waiting for my answer to his first question, he asked: 'Had yer much on?'

I answered, 'Not much', for I felt the ice very thin under my feet, never having heard of Minora until then, and was further saved by Helen asking: 'What's your fancy, dad?'

Then he told me in strict confidence to 'put a bit on Lemberg.'

That was how I got introduced to her people; and after that it became just a matter of 'going home with Nellie'.

All through the summer, life became very sweet indeed, and I whistled and sang as I walked behind Violet and Prince at the plough, with the tall trees all around in their summer greenery, and the lapwings nesting on the bare fallow; and I dreamed of a day when I should have saved up enough cash to take a little farm where Helen and I would live happily for ever and ever.

And then Martlemas drew near again. Martlemas, by the way, falls on 11th November and is the feast of St Martin, when, during the spell of fine weather that is usual at that period, the Martlemas Ox was killed and salted down for the winter. Nowadays, of course, the custom is knocked on the head, for no farmer in these days wants a whole ox salting down. So Martlemas is a thing of the past. Since the Great War and the passing of the Agricultural Wages Bill nothing has remained but memories of a Martlemas Fair, and the 'statutes' and the 'hirings', and the taking of 'fastening-pennies'.

Well, I came to my last day of my last year as a hired servant, for I was determined to chuck it and earn lots of money at the new colliery. I must have been optimistic, for I always tipped up most of my year's money to help mother along; so that little farm was yet a long way in front. It was not necessary to rise at four-thirty on leaving-day, but at that early hour we were out as usual, with our stable lanterns bobbing across the yard like Jack-o'-Lanterns. Such rubbing and scrubbing and combing out of manes you never saw, for a wagoner who is worth his salt never leaves his stable unkempt. Then, having fed and watered our horses and made their skins shine like velvet, we stood and gazed longingly at them, for you cannot leave the horse you have worked for a twelvemonth without just a tinge of regret, and be the place a good one or a bad, the horse has been your pal just the same.

So we stand and stare, while George carefully selects a piece of straw, which he starts chewing like a big, fat bullock. Presently he takes down the lantern from its cord fastened to the ceiling and, setting it on the corn-bin, proceeds to draw out his watch to see how the time is going. This is a longish job, for the watch fits tight in its little pocket in George's trousers, and the chain seems like a pulley-chain, and endless. Grasping the chain firmly in his right hand, he begins winding it round and round like a windlass until, no more chain being available, out comes the watch, like the bung of a beer-barrel. Holding it to the light, he says: 'Owf-past foive!'

So, with a goodbye glance at our horses, we go clamping in our heavy boots over the cobbled yard to our last breakfast.

May (the maid) looks very demure this morning as she brings the great milk saucepan off the fire and fills our basins. We had all been a jolly party, and the maid will find life quiet the week we are all away, though she may be able to stay in bed a little longer through not having to get our breakfast ready at the unearthly hour of five-thirty. (I wonder if any maid lays the breakfast at that hour today?) So we sit and talk and eat our fat bacon, discussing what to do with our holiday, until the boss comes in and, with a cough, says: 'Weel, lads, I reckon you want some money this morning?'

So he reckons up George's subs first, which don't quite tally with

George's reckonings, and after some arguing as to when he subbed this amount and that, the gaffer counts out a little pile of golden sovereigns, and George's year is paid for. Then he does the same with me, but with less arguing, for he wants me to stop on and be his head wagoner, having begged hard for the last few weeks for me to consider it. But I refuse to be persuaded, for I have other plans, and so I draw my pile of sovereigns, and he passes on to Jack.

After breakfast we yoke up the old galloway and take our boxes to the crossroads to be picked up by the carrier. Then we return with the cart, call on the shepherd's wife, who has been the farm servants' washer and mender from time immemorial, pay her the stipulated sovereign for our year's wash – the lad being charged half-price – and, mounting our cycles, take our leave of Woodland Farm.

Taken on the whole it was a jolly life, with little to trouble about, for boots and clothes were good and cheap in those days, and during Martlemas week the hireling got measured for his year's outfit, or paid for those that had been made during the year, and a good pair of cobbler-made boots could not be kicked to death in one year. After that, he spent his money in ale, and then returned to work for more.

Twelve

SUNSHINE AND SHADOW

WHAT A CHANGE I found in the old village after six years' absence. It seemed as though a town of bricks had been carried bodily through the air and dropped on Little Norwood, leaving bits of stone cottages showing here and there. The two inns had been done up, while a miners' institute and a fish-and-chip shop showed how greatly Little Norwood was developing. We were progressing, socially and materially, and no longer dared Sam Tracey – you will remember Sam, it was he who won ten pounds on Rock Sand – claim his own particular corner of the long settle in the Jug and Glass; whilst the sexton's opinion on matters genealogical had become of no account, owing to the hybrid stock that was fast growing up. Ben Cobb's carrier-cart rusted under its shed, and old Jasper, instead of transporting passengers to town, now carted bricks on the new building sites. Two farmsteads had entirely disappeared to make room for shops, and a branch of the Midland Bank now flaunted its front where once had stood a cowshed. I remember a laburnum used to bloom at the corner of the penthouse that was fowl-house and coal-place combined, and is now – Lord, help us! – a window of gaudy jewellery with 'Unredeemed pledges' pasted across on a slip of paper.

A model village, with church, chapels and a fine new council school had sprung up where oats and wheat and bailey had followed each other in about a dozen different fields. I lived in the 'model' after I got wed, and can say from experience that a model colliery village is an ideal place in which to live if you want to see all the different shades of life. There is no half-and-half measure about a collier; either he is intensely religious, or intensely the opposite, and both classes are good-hearted and neighbourly to the last degree.

The only fault to find with living in a colliery village is in rather startling movements that take place among inanimate objects. For instance, each block of houses, when built, is surrounded by a low brick wall, with a little gate leading to each house, but for some unaccountable reason the copings wander away off the wall-top; no one takes them off, and no one sees them go – they just go. The same thing happens to the yard gates, but usually these disappear during the excitement of a coal strike. The most curious thing I found was the movement amongst clothes posts. These have a strange fancy for wandering, and the first item on wash day was to see if the clothes post was there. Several times I fetched our clothes post from the end of the row, where it would be hiding behind hand-carts, broken bed heads, dog kennels, or some like bit of furniture beloved of colliers. There was never any argument about getting it back, whichever house it wandered to. The people were surprised to see it there, and had no idea how it came. Providing you can get used to these little happenings, life in a 'model' is well enough.

But to get back to my story. I left farm service 24th November 1910 full of hopes at making a start straight away at the colliery, but it was the spring of 1912 before I got set on. In the meantime I got a carter's job on the buildings at a pound per week, out of which I paid mother sixteen shillings for my board and keep; the usual rate is fourteen shillings, but then a lad cannot be 'shinny' with his own mother. Four shillings pocket-money wasn't bad in those days, when cigarettes were ten for threepence and tobacco fourpence per ounce. But still it wasn't enough for my purpose, and often, after a trip to town especially, I found there was nothing left to my banking account. So I tried carrying bricks; but, bless yer life! The Lord never intended my head to ram eight bricks at a time up a ladder to suit any builder or contractor, so I chucked it and went back to horse driving.

Then the new pit opened out, and I got a job as labourer, the pre-War pay being four shillings and sixpence per shift from six a.m. to five p.m., with knocking off time at one on Saturday. I now felt more satisfied, and Helen and that little place of our own seemed much nearer. The engine-wright took some notice of me, as he did of anyone who looked like work, and put me on boiler firing at five shillings per shift of eight hours and seven days a week.

I was rising rapidly, and when in May 1914 the colliery company started up a coking-plant I was given the opportunity of having a good job there. I was never an opportunist by any means, and but for the engine-wright might have stayed at the heavy job of boiler firing. He offered me a good job in the sulphate-house, and I, never having heard of such a place as a sulphate-house, and knowing nothing about coke ovens, was going to decline, when he, in his blunt way, said: 'Don't be a dam' fooil, nobody knows how till they try, and these jobs aren't picked up i' the street!'

So I became a sulphate-house attendant, because the engine-wright had to look up a few likely men for the main jobs; and there I stayed until the 1921 coal strike.

'Ah!' you say; 'one of the indispensables who got out of the War, eh?' No. It was just chance. I rushed off with a number of other lads from the coke ovens, eager to be in what seemed a great adventure in those early days. But too many of us had gone at once, leaving the ovens at a standstill. So I, along with one or two more skilled and semi-skilled by-product men, were sent back to wait until called for. And so fate, that sent so many poor lads out, kept me back; and whether it was to my discredit or not, I had no zeal for fighting after 1915.

At Christmas time, 1914, one of Helen's brothers was home on leave before being drafted out to France along with his master, and we had a rare fuddle. She had three brothers who were grooms to different gentlemen, and they all joined up in the early days. They were fine horsemen, and as everyone in those days had splendid old-fashioned ideas of the glories of war, their great hope was of one day taking part in a dashing cavalry charge. But that Christmas is most memorable to me because Helen gave her consent to our marriage.

I was now twenty-four, and my wage two pounds per week. We had waited five years, and as neither of us could see any reason for waiting longer, we got married. There was only one hitch to my carefully worked-out plans. Mother and Helen had always got on very well together whenever I brought her home, and mother made her more than welcome. But when I suggested my plan of the three of us living in one house, mother put her foot down very firmly, and, amongst other things, said: 'Though she couldn't wish me wed to a better wench, there couldn't be two missis's in one house', that 'it wouldn't be fair to Helen', and 'that a lass wants a house of her own and doesn't want to be saddled wi' her mother -i'-law'.

All of which was no doubt wise counsel, though I couldn't see it at the time, and only saw the extra expense of keeping two homes where one might have served. However, on 3rd February 1915, Helen became mine, and a red-brick house in a sombre street became a 'little place', because Helen was there; and because of a pair of soft-grey eyes and waving brown hair that shared my table, I sang like a farmer's boy, for it seemed as though a whole eternity of happiness lay before us.

What fun we had in those early housekeeping days. I hadn't saved a deal of money, so we just built our nest bit by bit, like the birds. And a cosy nest she made it, I can tell you. Such planning and scheming of what we should get next, and most of it second-hand, for we visited sales and auction rooms and had a gay old time that first summer, with the result we got much better quality than our purse could have afforded at the smart furniture shops, and everything was paid for before it came into the house.

We indulged in one extravagance during the next year. Because of my love of books we bought the Dickens's Library, which was then being widely advertised, and the pleasure we got out of them was well worth the expense. I used to read passages aloud to Helen while she sat at her sewing – she not being a great reader – and thereby got double pleasure in becoming acquainted with Pickwick, Sairy Gamp, Mark Tapley and all those lovable people; and at the same time got the pleasure of hearing

Helen's laughter as I read of some amusing character. They were great days, and sometimes when I looked across at that lovely head bent over her sewing I used to wonder how it all came about, that I, a farm-joskin, should be possessed of so much wealth of happiness in a world full of sorrow.

In October 1916 our daughter was born, and one Sunday afternoon we had that most important event in the life of a young married couple – the first christening party. It isn't possible for a farmhand to put down on paper the joy and happiness of that little party. How we used the front-room for the occasion because the front-room was only used on special occasions, and how two grandmothers shared the infant between them while Helen did the honours of the tea-table. How they kept saying: 'Sit ye down a bit, lassie; let 'em wait o' theirsels a bit! Now don't ye be too venturesome!'

How Helen had to be venturesome, for this was her day. And if only you'd have seen her pouring out the tea and saying, 'Sugar, Harry?' to her brother-in-law, and 'How many?' to her married sister, and asking her girlfriend who stood godmother how she liked our tea-service, because it was a wedding present from the Hall, and how she handed round the cheesecakes and tarts made by the newly made grandmothers, and the way she got up to fill the teapot for the second round, and how she patted her hair before the glass – for she was very vain that afternoon – and how her cheeks had just a tinge of colour the first time for weeks. Unless you had been there to see, I cannot make you understand what an important affair was that first christening, and what an important person was Helen.

After tea our visitors had to be shown our nest, even to the hang of the window curtains and the pattern of the wallpaper; and then the infant had to be undressed and fed, and Helen modestly turned aside her rocker. We tried to talk about wheat, or work, or war; but it was ladies' night, and the talk would get back to babies. Then they all went home, and I was left with Helen – and Margaret.

In August 1918 our son was born, and we christened him William after both his grandfathers. Helen came down looking very pale, for she was never very robust, and was some time in getting on her feet again. However, in 1919 we were able to join in the peace celebrations and all the happy do's that were being held in the village. I was prospering, and now that the War was over we turned our thoughts once more to that little place of our own.

We both preferred the country, and wanted to get away from the busy colliery village and take a house with at least a garden attached to it. We were never over-careful or near about saving money, we just enjoyed the good things in life without running into debt. But money was plentiful towards the end of the War, and by Helen's good housekeeping we had put by nearly one hundred pounds.

In 1920 a little holding came to let. It was only a couple of acres, but was within easy reach of the pit. I knew the owner, and everything seemed to be working right-hand first, for I could nicely manage a few pigs and poultry on two acres. There was a splendid garden with fruit trees, too, and I could still carry on with my work at the ovens. Helen fell in love with the house and flower garden, and there was no end to the rosy dreams we had of the future and the castles we built.

In March she was stricken down with flu, and though the doctor and nurses worked hard to save her she just faded away like a cropped flower. I watched her helplessly; I prayed to God, and all the women that came to help, to save her for me, but it was no use. My little lassie faded away, and left me with all the meaning gone out of my world.

My life was now empty, useless, and after we had laid her to rest I packed up our home and went to live at home with mother. The years that followed were barren and uninteresting to talk about. The coal strike in 1921 about cleared out my savings, and I didn't care a hang what became of them now, for I'd finished with schemes and castles, and just drifted along like a ship that had lost its rudder.

But my troubles showed what warm-hearted friends I had got, and what splendid folk there are in colliery villages when a chap's down, and how they share his troubles and try to make things as easy as possible by little acts of sympathy. I read quite a lot at that time, too, through a friend encouraging me to read Shakespeare and the plays of other authors, both past and present, so that I became interested for the first time in drama and the stage, and by degrees took my mind off my own troubles and left a loop-hole for a little light to filter through. But I couldn't make out the riddle of life, and why this happened, or for what purpose was anything. I got sick of Little Norwood, with its rapid changes. So when slack times came along after the strike I wandered back to the land.

I will jump those barren years and start again with the year 1925, and if the rest of my story is flippant at times it is because I have swallowed the philosophy of Omar Khayyám, and, unable to piece life together into any satisfactory shape, intend henceforth 'to make a jest of that which makes as much of me.'

Thirteen

A FRESH START

ON 8TH JANUARY 1925 I STARTED LIFE again as a farm labourer. I am
certain about the date because since then I have kept my diary pretty
regular. And as my own village held nothing but buried hopes I took a job
on a dairy farm near Sheffield.

I had married again, my second wife being a young woman named
Elizabeth, with a taste for literature greater than my own, and a rare hand
at making pastries. She can quote Shakespeare, chapter and verse, and turns
out excellent crumpets, which is all I now ask of life. So I loaded up my
furniture on a lorry on 8th January, put my wife and kiddies in the cab with
the driver, and rode myself atop of my furniture. I was glad to get away,
and yet as I rode along on top of the lorry and saw the receding village and
the old familiar landmarks, I felt very wretched and low-spirited, and by
the time the old grey church had disappeared from view I was crying like
a child. It was a daft thing for a great fellow of thirty-four to be pewling
like an infant, but I just couldn't help it. I crouched amongst my household
treasures and wept. So that's that; and now for happier things.

The farm I went to was nearly all grassland, and, as I had never worked
on a dairy farm, but had always been used to horse work, ploughing and
harrowing and such like, I didn't settle down very well at first. We had
thirty-five cows to milk morning and night, after which I had to clean out
the sheds, feed a bunch of calves and a herd of pigs, carry in hay and corn
for next day's ration, and tidy up the yard in my spare time. I never had
any spare time, and my boyhood days at Hill-top Farm were a holiday

compared with what I was expected to do at this place. My hours were supposed to be from six to six, with half a day off each week on account of dairying requiring a full day on Sunday. I was lucky if I got finished by seven, including Saturday and Sunday night, and as for half-days, I gave them up as a bad job.

The chief reason for being late at night lay with the boss. He couldn't keep his men, for he was the most over-bearing little wretch I ever came across; if he ever heard of the Agricultural Wages Board it was evident they had never heard of him. It was amusing really, the way he used to carry on, as though the earth was for him to walk upon; and we were bits of earth. When we had a full staff – which we never had all the time I was there – there was a cowman, horseman, roundsman, and two milk lads. But – alas for getting finished in decent time! – there was always either a man or a lad short. I believe I got sacked on an average of once a month, but I was never one to fear a barking dog, and as for his sacking anyone, it seemed quite unnecessary, for they never stayed long enough to be sacked. So I stuck it until I should hear of something better. And somehow he gave up sacking me as a bad job, and one Saturday there was only the two milk boys and myself left to look after the cattle.

He raised my wage from two pounds to forty-five shillings if I would promise not to jack-up and not answer back when spoken to. The last request was difficult, and looking back in my diary I find many entries like this: 'Had a rare bust up today'; 'Seven-thirty when I came home tonight'; 'Expected a new cowman this week, but he has sent back word.' But – usually I contented myself with a sarcastic verse like this:

The mighty Julius Caesar blew a blast upon his horn,
   Just to let us know he would be if he could.
And he raises up his bristles like a hedgehog in the
     thorn
Or a gadfly out for some poor sinner's blood.
   And we take it in with awe
   As we wilt beneath his 'jaw',
Though we don't know what it's for or what
     about.

So I dismiss him; for I want to say what a pleasant job it is being a milk-roundsman, and what a highly important job too, for I was engaged as a roundsman, though I was more often cowman and horseman combined. Not many people realise the tact and diplomacy required to be a successful purveyor of milk, and how, though the butcher and baker may call at any hour, the milk must be there to the minute, or the whole domestic arrangements are upset. It requires great tact to manage a milk round, and only by careful study of each individual householder can one hope to become a successful milk-seller. That I was successful is due, not to any merit of my own, but to the genial good-natured mistresses and maids who took in the milk, and were always very nice about it when I splashed a wee drop on their clean doorstep. Of course, it's quite different nowadays with this bottled milk, and there's no excuse for a friendly word with the maid or mistress; but in those days, incredible as it may seem, I always sized up the personality of the mistress by the pattern on her milk bowl or jug.

There's big jugs and little jugs, an' jugs wi' fancy trimmin'.
There's jolly jugs wi' curly lugs, an' bowls a duck might swim in.
There's sober brown, an' Derby Crown, an' jugs inclined to slimmin'.
But every jug resembles close the features o' the wimmin.

This may sound disrespectful to the ladies of Sheffield, to whom I apologise. In certain districts, too, you may tell by the inside of the jug what the family partook for supper the fore-night. But that remark didn't apply to my customers. It was a residential district, and though I thought them a bit starchy at first, I soon found them the jolliest and most pleasant people to get along with. I had a glorious time among the 'upper ten' at Sheffield, and one thing I must say, going round with milk in the suburbs is an education almost equal to a year at college. Between the mistress and maid you are primed with the knowledge of the universe, while the questions that are asked would qualify a milkman for a bobby's job or an editor's chair, could he but answer one-half of them.

So I found life very pleasant once again, in spite of the boss's churlishness, and learned at the back doors of the great to take an interest in grand opera, and who were the stars in *The Nibelungenlied* at the Lyceum. From those of a dramatic turn I gathered a smattering of the stage of Bernard Shaw and Noel Coward, while another type knew all the latest books, hot from the press – these were younger people, with modern furniture and hygienic babies. But they were all very pleasant to talk to, though I liked best to chat with the old retired couples who knew their Shakespeare and quoted Pope and Browning while they trained rambler roses and clipped privet hedges, and greeted me with: 'Here comes our philosophical milkman.'

And so at the back door of society I travelled from Shakespeare to the latest novelist, and learned everyone's opinion on politics, golf, boat-races, rearing of infants and poultry, without disclosing the fact that I was an uncultured farm labourer; for a roundsman, however humble, must appear informed to the ladies at the back door.

One of my customers was a devout worshipper at a very fashionable church in town, and on her recommendation I went one Sunday to evening service. For once in a way I finished work in time. I went to the church and looked round. It was a sight to see. People drove up in fine motor cars; fathers in black coats and silk hats led fur-coated mothers and silk-stockinged daughters into the church, each clutching to her breast a dainty satchel and prayer book. I was rather awed by it all, and felt a bit out of place, for it wasn't anything like our village church, or the chapel, but I sat well at the end of a pew so as not to show up amongst such stylish dress. That summer night was my first opportunity of attending a place of worship since going to Sheffield.

Two of my customers lived up a row with passages leading to the back, one at each side of the passage. The man on his side blew very hard on a cornet; the lady's dog howled very hard on the other side. When I called on the cornet-player he would say, 'I wish you'd shoot that dam'd dog, milkman!' and when I called on the lady she poured into my ear the distresses of living next door to a cornet-player who disturbed poor Sancho. Like a good milkman, I sympathised with both. So I trotted from door to door, giving advice on babies, ailing dogs, and certainties for the big race. I had cigarettes given me, and cakes and chocolates, and whenever I was off the round for a while – until the new cowman or horseman came – on my return I was greeted with, 'Why, it's our old milkman this morning!'; or, 'This is nice; to have your grin showing round again!' Indeed, they were the nicest, jolliest people I have ever met anywhere, and I had thought them terribly starchy when first I started going round.

I got a pleasant surprise at Christmas. I expected getting a few tips and Christmas farings, but I little thought I would have five pounds given to me, besides lots of cigarettes, cigars, mince pies and drinks. Perhaps these seem trifling things to write about, but to me these little kindnesses are the most important things in life, and are the seasoning that makes life palatable. And nowhere, when I was on my rounds, did I run across that much-talked-of class distinction or snobbishness – only a real desire to goodwill and friendliness.

And now, back to the farm. The great fault with the gaffer was he didn't talk with his men; he talked at them, which was a mistake, for a farm man who knows his job needs no talking at, but will do his work better for a boss who talks with him. Now, each Tuesday and Thursday we fetched a load of brewer's grains from the malt kilns in town – wet grains being very good for milk production – and one day the boss put a hundred eggs in a box for me to deliver at a shop in town. Instead of using a proper egg-crate he packed them in chaff, and as the top eggs looked bare I suggested covering them with more chaff. A boss has a right to his own opinion, but I didn't like the short way in which he said: 'Mind your own business, and get off!'

So off I got, with a hundred eggs on an empty block-dray with no springs, and the street where I had to leave them was paved with rough stone setts. I carried the box on my knee when I got to the bumpy part and let the horse drive itself. But it was terribly jolty, and I saw the chaff riddling down lower and lower, while the eggs seemed to bob higher and higher, and I knew something was going to happen to those eggs before they got much older. Then the front wheel dropped in a grate-hole and the eggs settled down with a gentle hush. When I handed the box to the shop keeper he just stared hard and said: 'What's this?' I replied: 'It's not unlike an omelette, mister!' The boss and I had a few words later.

I often wonder what became of all the milk boys who rode in the cart with me for a little while and then disappeared. By the good start they made in book-keeping and accountancy they will probably by now have developed into cashiers or bank managers. We had two milk boys sometimes. Often we had less, and it used to work out like this. Following an advertisement in the *Sheffield Daily Telegraph* there would be a glut of would-be milk boys for a day or two. After a careful selection by the boss and the missus the boys would be reduced to one, and he was taught the art of delivering milk to the customers and delivering certain payments to the boss, for which he received in wage the sum of six shillings per week, plus his board and bed. That, then, was the order of his coming. Before his hasty departure, the milk boy always seemed to have plenty of chocolate and cigarettes, and as I couldn't see this being done on six shillings a week I would question the lad and warn the boss, without making either party see sense. Then some Sunday morning the boss would come tearing into the cowshed, asking: 'Is Jack here?'

Jack wouldn't be here, and if he didn't turn up on Monday morning we knew then he had absconded and someone's milk account was out of order. Sometimes he was found, and the money refunded; sometimes his whereabouts were unknown, and we had another influx of milk boys for a day or two.

Well, that's how we carried on, and I wouldn't have stayed so long myself but for the fact that I liked that part of the country and found the suburban dwellers of Sheffield such a pleasant crowd to get along with. In January 1936 we had a sale, and I stayed on with the new tenant.

I found in him quite a change from my former master. He was bluff, fat, and easy-going, while the other had been opposite in all three points. He and his wife were very easy folk to get on with; but, as they had three sons of milk-delivering age, I didn't get on the round quite so often, and was horseman the whole time I was there.

The cowman was a rough, bent-axled old chap who went by the name of Judd. He wore a long coat with two large buttons in the rear, a coat that seemed to have come off a respectable family. Whenever he felt 'a bit o' cow'd coming on' he drank large quantities of rum, and he always had a cold coming on. But he was a good cowman, and had been with the boss a good many years, and was very critical about what sort of cattle came into the shed. The gaffer, like most farmers, was keen on snapping up doubtful bargains. Whenever a sorry-looking specimen came in, Judd eyed it over with a critical eye, while the quid of 'bacca' worked round and round in his mouth. Then he would spit across the floor and say: 'Sho's not a milker! No, sho bain't owt of a milker, maister!'

The boss would answer: 'Yar, mun, sho'll be a ewesful beast when sho picks up a bit!'

'Aye! sho will, and sho'll want pickin' up afore long, maister, i' my opinion.'

'Nay, mun, sho wonner dee, sho wonner dee. Sho's too bright in t' eye to go wrong.'

They would then both begin pinching the cow's skin to see if there was slack enough to put any flesh underneath, and Judd would declare 'sho were hide-bun', while the gaffer was equally certain 'sho any wanted a bit o' good keep to mak' a cow of her.'

I wonder what the cow thinks about it all, for cows do think in their way, and stare with a bewildered sort of look, while its new owner pinches its skin, draws out its teats, and turns it about to see if it can stand on all four legs.

Beside Judd, we had a long, lanky youth, named Charlie, who worked for us. He was a native of the moors, and should have stayed there, for he was too 'gaumless' to live in the town. He took to drinking rum along with Judd. And one Monday morning, after having soaked himself well with drink during the weekend, he jumped into the lake and got an all-round soak, after first writing a farewell message to all his friends and pinning it on the yard gate, with this inscription: 'You will find my body at the bottom of the lake. Goodbye. Charlie.'

We did not find his body at the bottom of the lake, as he seemed to have changed his mind after drinking a quantity of water, and was found lying, exhausted, on the bank. The police were called, and they, after emptying the water out of Charlie back into the lake, took him in a waiting ambulance to an institution known to Sheffielders as Firvale. A fortnight later he returned (under supervision), and was told to keep out of pubs.

He managed very well for quite a time. And then one Saturday night I called in on one myself, and there was Charlie, 'laking' at darts with a big hefty forgeman. The forgeman had just thrown, getting ten and a four, while one arrow had fallen to the ground. He stooped to pick it up, while our 'gaumless' Charlie shoved up his sleeve for a throw. The next thing I saw was the arrow sticking up as pert as a cock-sparrow in the forgeman's neck; he was wearing a thick muffler, or it might have been much worse. However, I didn't like the look of his eye as he went out to have his neck seen to, and I tried to persuade Charlie to come home. But he was always a gaumless youth, and said he 'were entitled to another throw because Harry had baulked his aim.'

I tried to drag him out; but couldn't without causing a disturbance, and the rest of the company said, 'Let him stop!' so I left him there and hoped for the best. I never saw him afterwards, for the probation officer found him work on the roads in one of the moorland villages, but they say he looked a nice pickle after Harry came back.

Talking about the moorland villages reminds me of a trip I took along with old Judd to fetch a load of trussed hay, and what a journey it was. Farmers generally are a queer lot, and will argue all day over sixpence, swearing they 'won't bate a copper'; and then the one who wins the 'tanner' gives the other man a shilling back for luck. That's what they call 'coming it'. Our gaffer said of a neighbour he was 'trying to come it' by offering him a stack of good meadow hay at forty-five shillings a ton, so he bought a stack of inferior hay at forty shillings, the stack being about five miles away on the moors. It would cost fifty shillings a ton to get it home, but that didn't matter; he had turned the tables and 'come it' over the other man.

So Judd and I set off one morning to fetch the first load, with old Bonnie on the dray. No doubt it would have been a pleasant outing on a fine day, but the fog was so thick you couldn't see more than twenty yards ahead. A dreary road on a day like this, with a cold rain coming down through the fog, and no sound of life but the splash-splosh of Bonnie's hoofs and the jingle of harness chains and great splashes of rain beating down on the dray boards and, above all, Judd muttering curses on the weather; I should have mentioned before that Judd was a fine swearer. There was no sight to see but little stone walls and whin bushes, with occasionally a small farmstead looming through the mist. I could get no information out of Judd concerning any of these little places, for, whenever I asked, he just stopped swearing at the rain for a moment and swore at the little places.

At noon we drew into the yard of a little pub-cum-farm perched on the top of a high hill, and Judd said this was it; so, being fairly soaked with rain, we went inside for a bite of 'snap' before starting to truss our hay. It was a nice little inn, with curtains to the windows, and glad I was to get out of the rain for a while and watch my trousers steam before a cheery tap-room fire, while big splashes of rain trickled down the windowpanes in the foggy outside. It was such a relief to get under cover that even Judd enjoyed it without swearing, and after knocking off a great 'gollop o' rum to keep cow'd out', settled down to drink beer like an ordinary farm hand. We had got nicely thawed when the landlord came in, and, knowing Judd, as did most landlords, asked: 'An yer come for that hay, Judd, lad?'

Judd growled 'Arr!' and gently swore.

The landlord then explained: 'Weel, mun, the stack is na' at whoam. It's a bit of a stack I built i' the field, mebbe a mile awa', mebbe a bit less, but ye canna' miss it; if this fog lifts ye can see fra' the wa' end as ye turn by. But it's a rare day ye've picked to truss hay, for sure!'

Then Judd made up for all the times when he hadn't sworn, and what he said would have turned any ordinary man's beer on his stomach, and if I tried to write it down it would dry my ink up. But it was no use swearing; so out we had to go. And I know of no worse desolation and discomfort than to be perched atop of a haystack on these bleak Derbyshire hills, when everything seems lost in fog and rain.

But we went in fine weather, too; and it's wonderful the lovely scenery that encircles grimy old Sheffield. Once or twice I met Chris in the tap room. He was a bit of a character – the village wit, you might call him – one of those merry sort who prefer to poke fun at themselves than at other people. It was said of him that when the price of flour was going up during the Great War, Chris remarked to his tap-room friends: 'Weel, afore I'll pay half a crown a stone for flour I'll eat dry bread!' It was a daft thing to say, but it takes a wit to say it.

One day he had been out rabbiting, and coming home with his catch in a bag he met a friend who asked: 'How many have you caught?' To which Chris replied: 'If tha' can guess how many rabbits I have in this bag, I'll gie yer all t' five of 'em.' 'Five,' answered his friend. 'Ah, someb'dy must ha' telled ye!' and Chris walked away. Which may be true, or just a village tale.

The gaffer had a bit of land on the plough right out on the moors. It was too far away from home to be worked properly and too far from the manure heap to grow much produce; but that summer I put it in with potatoes, taking my dinner along and staying in the field all day. Sitting under a stonewall at dinner-time, what a sight it was, mile upon mile of uninterrupted view of field and meadow, and gently rising hills with little farmsteads dotted here and there. At my back was a grim and mighty hill, all purple-topped, and though the country had no leafy woods, it had a stream, which made music, all its own.

However, there were certain disadvantages to living any longer at this farm. The cottage we lived in was not merely damp, the walls ran with water, and the 1926 summer being very wet made it worse, whilst the coal strike made it difficult to keep the house warm. Another little difficulty was rats, 'Great rats, small rats, lean rats, brawny rats'; we had a plague of them that wet summer, and though we tried poison and cats, still they came. My missus and I would be sitting by the fire after the kiddies were put to bed, and there would come that scrape, scrape, scrape at doors, under the hearthstone, and in the roof. We came to the conclusion that either the rats or we must go. So we left, in favour of the oldest tenants. In November our youngest child was born, and, as the cottage was unhealthy for children, I began looking out for a fresh pasture so soon as ever my wife got on her feet again. It was not until after Christmas that I got satisfied, and in January 1927 we settled down with a farmer near to Worksop.

Fourteen

A COWMAN'S DIARY

I BEGAN WORK WITH MY PRESENT EMPLOYER on 1st February 1927. And as he may read what I have to say about him, he being more widely read than most farmers, I must be careful!

The best way to describe my life from now onwards will be to copy little bits from my diaries. My first entry was: 'Rise at six, milk till seven-thirty, breakfast, take milk to town, do various bits of shopping.'

Later on it reads like this: 'The boss chuntered this morning because I was late getting back with the milk cart. Shall tell him off one of these days, see if I don't. I'm a cowman, I am, not a bally steam engine. Got hindered in this kind of way. Nellie gave me eightpence to bring two loaves for the missus. Mrs Moss gave me one shilling and eightpence for a tin of Neaves's Food (evidently she's decided to give this one the bottle), Mrs Tracey sixpence for a dozen clothes pegs and a penn'orth o' blue, and our Lizzie a pound o' pie meat for today's dinner.'

Being a cowman means that you have no certain job in between milking times, consequently I get a lot of what we call dodging-about jobs; that is, if you see a job coming, dodge it. This afternoon the missus asked me to go down the cellar as the barrel needed tilting. Well, I'm always willing to oblige if it's serious, so I tilted the barrel, eased the spile peg, and got a steady flow of beer.

The missus is a very good sort if you do any little jobs for her, and usually has a few mince pies on the cellar head which come in handy on barrel-tilting occasions. The boss is greatly taken up with grand opera, and on several occasions he has taken me to Sheffield to see, first the British National Opera, and, more recently, the Carl Rosa. In this way I have learnt to appreciate first-class music.

Once or twice we went to farm sales – they were in the springtime – setting off after dinner and getting home again by milking-time. It is a pity how some of the farmers have had to give up after being on the farm for several generations, and worse still is the extinction of several big country mansions and the splitting up of large estates.

And so I come to this entry: 'Been with the boss to a farm sale this afternoon. There is a saying round here that every farm should have a sale or a fire once in ten years to clear away the rubbish.'

I quite agree. Nothing less than a fire or a sale would induce a farmer to clear his place of old scrap. He collects old harness, broken carts and worn-out implements with the persistence of a stamp collector. He will chase a broken-wheeled wagon with the rage of a butterfly pursuer. And all for why? 'It might come in handy,' he says. For that reason the lumber heap grows and grows, more and more rubbish is added, until a fire becomes a necessity to relieve him of things put by and forgotten.

The farm we went to hadn't changed hands for five generations, neither had it known a fire for a hundred years at the least. What an accumulation on its lumber heap! I made for the corn-chamber steps; the starting point of every sale on a farm. This chamber is more interesting than the outside lumber heap, and on sale day is the calendar of the farm's progress throughout all generations. At the far end lie buried the broken tools of the first generation; things that might have come in handy, but never did.

The auctioneer, a man in a check suit and brown leggings, had got well into the family affairs when I arrived. Standing on the top step he had rattled off as fast as they were passed out, a collection of broken harness, whips, spuds, hoes, cricket bat, fishing rods and ditching tools. An old muzzleloader, with ramrod and powder-flask complete, was being passed out, which shows he had got down to grandfather's remains at the least. Some dibbling irons and a set of threshing flails followed, while an ancient, worm-eaten cheese-press wobbled a second in the doorway, and collapsed. We had got down to great-grandfather's remains, and, somehow, it seemed out of place to lay hands on them. An old wheel came out that had once been a spinning-frame, and had been laid by in the dust of old forgotten things until this agricultural depression brought it to light. Well, I've been to a farm sale, but I can't say much about it; except that the lumber heap is the most interesting and, at the same time, the most disturbing part about it.

Up to now I haven't mentioned anything about work. I do a bit sometimes, though I would have you understand a farm labourer's life is not now the down-trodden, all bed-and-work existence of popular imagination. 'Today we have been threshing wheat, and a bleak east wind has blown down the stack-yard all day, swirling the chaff and straw in exasperating eddies away from the threshing-machine.' Clouds of smoke would swoop down and engulf the machine and men in its choking fumes. It would lift again, veering north-east, revealing a dozen swarthy figures begrimed in dust and smoke. It would come back again, sweeping round the corner of the stack, catch up a column of chaff and spin it merrily across the yard. Only the two men on the stack can keep fairly free from dust, as they pass the sheaves on to the drum. The drum becomes a god to the band-cutter and the feeder, who bend over his wide-open jaws, thrusting sheaves into his rapacious belly, while he coughs and moans, belching out clouds of dust from his fearful lungs. So they bend over, and feed and feed, as though their lives were dedicated to the service of a hungry god. At the straw end its bond slaves carry away the emptied straw, now neatly tied up in bottles, and build a stack in defiance of the east wind, which tries the corner-stones of their building. At the corn end the yellow grain comes pouring down over a screen, the good wheat falling into eighteen-stone bags, to be carried away by a hefty high priest into the granary. The chaff lad is buried in the off-scourings of the mighty god, as he rakes and rakes from under the monster's belly, and finishes up by being smothered in chaff from his boots to his hair. And so the great god groans and grunts and belches, while his devotees bow and scrape before him in hopeless adoration, and I, in my spare time, join in, giving a hand with the straw until three o'clock milking-time.

After threshing there is the corn to deliver in town, either to the miller or the maltster. I can't help noticing the change that has come over the horse lads of today. Not a bit of pride in their horses, not a ribbon nor a brass, nor the harness cleaned up, to show they were going a-teaming; whereas at one time o' day a wagoner wouldn't for very shame take a pair of horses on the road unless he had a bit of 'caddis' in their tails and a clean face-piece for each horse. But fashions change, and most of them for the better, so that nowadays, when we weed our corn or hoe turnips, we get the older generation talking of their prowess at the plough or at stacking, while the youngsters talk about the latest films, and the galaxy of stars that twinkle on the screen and the football field.

But to get back to work. The wagoner is delivering the wheat to town and, the land being frost bound, the other chaps are busy leading manure. Carting manure is not the unpleasant job anyone might suppose, and this frosty weather gives it quite a healthy smell. The only fault with manure leading is when taking off your boots at night. Not the stink! Though they may buzz a little if placed near the fire. The fault is you may have frost in your feet through standing on hot manure. But this weather is delicious. Everyone is 'waffing' their arms to keep the blood from freezing in their finger-ends. Lovely weather, too, when the sun gets out, glittering the hedges and the frozen puddles along the lane, and your breath comes steamy like a singing kettle. And how sweet is the smell of tobacco on a frosty morning.

We are orphans for the next few days, the boss and missus having gone away for Easter to recuperate after his accident; we were bandaging a cow's foot when it kicked, injuring the boss's hand severely. I am at present custodian of the farmhouse.

This morning, after feeding the pigs and cows and cleaning them out, I swilled the cowhouse floor, mended a pig-trough, got some hay in for the night, and filled in my spare time setting posts and rails round the orchard.

(While the boss was away I sold two pigs for fifty shillings, and whether I did anything else noteworthy is not on record, so this is the day after the boss's return.)

I was digging out soft holes in the orchard in my spare time, when the boss came strolling up.

'Yer not getting on very fast,' says he; but that being the usual opening remark of a farmer to his men, I didn't take much heed.

'If I'd stayed away much longer, work would ha' come to a standstill. How much longer is this bit of a job going to last?' he asked.

'If you'd ha' stayed away much longer job uld ha' been finished wi'out yer!' I answered, going on with my digging.

'Hem! Well, 'ere's a bit o' 'bacca I've brought yer, for looking after things while we were away.' So I gave over digging to thank him for the ''bacca'.

He goes on: 'I see you've sold a couple o' pigs.'

I answered: 'Yes, fifty bob; couldn't get no more!'

Then he gives me two shillings and sixpence for luck, and, telling me to 'ram into it', goes off to inspect the other chaps.

When he'd gone I had a smoke, just to try his tobacco, and 'rammed in' at my post hole, thinking what a pleasant world this is to live in. Presently I unearthed a cow's skull that had lain buried there for years, and it set my mind working in another direction, so that I forgot all about the boss and little pigs and 'ramming in'. It's wonderful what turns up in your mind while you're at work. As I tossed the cow's head out of the hole I was immediately transported to the churchyard scene in *Hamlet*.

So I mused on Shakespeare and dug out post holes in the orchard fence until the boss came back and, viewing my labours, said: 'Nah yer shaping! Yer getting on wi' the job now!'

I had dug one hole less than on the previous day, but then farmers are like that.

The black sow farrowed this weekend. A big, ungainly creature, she ought to have been 'fed off' this winter. Started off with fourteen followers to her credit, but evidently she believes in the restriction of families, for she usually squashes one out of existence every time she lays down. She has now six left, and they go one by one. The pigman calls her 'Marry Stoops', and every time a little pig starts squealing you hear him running to the rescue – half a minute too late.

Then the springtime came, greening the lane with hemlock and cow parsley and setting the blackies whistling.

'Nah then!' said the boss as I was setting off to town, 'I want yer back quick; we're going to get busy, and I've a nice easy job waiting for ye.'

That's the worst of my life. I've always been doing odd jobs ever since I left school.

Ralph had chisel-harrowed the twelve-acre and got a good mould ready for oats; so today he has been drilling while I follow after with the light harrows, along with the milk horse and old Captain. But it's pleasant to be walking over the good brown earth, and Dick (the milk horse) enjoys it too. He is glad to be rid of the cart and the rattle of wheels, and steps out jauntily on the soft earth. The sun and clouds race each other over the fields, the peewits swirl around, watching with interest the corn drill hiding good oats in the soil. The rooks settle warily at a safe distance and begin to dig, until Rover sees them and gives chase in a whirl of dust. The rooks rise in a black cloud and exclaim noisily about it from the next field until Rover lies down again and they return to their digging. It's good to be out in the fields when the sun shines, and though I am not now a horseman, I get these harrowing jobs occasionally.

Sometimes we have domestic upsets, like this. 'Was milking Emlyn tonight when Sara, who stands next, gave me a playful push. Emlyn didn't like it so pushed me back again. Sara passed me back to Emlyn, and Emlyn passed me back to Sara, and so they kept on until I rolled into the manger.' It's a habit with some cows, and one gets used to it. It is no use crying over spilt milk, and most of the cows are very quiet and well-behaved. We have twelve in full milk, with several 'strippers' and 'in-calfers'.

I like a cow to have a nice name, and these are a few of the names. Janet, Ruth, Daphne, Bluebell, Daisy, Blackbird, Trilby, Julia, Sara, Emlyn and

Judith. The bull has no particular name, but is generally referred to as Billy or 'Owd Bill'. He has a playful habit of 'coming after' when he sees anyone in his grass field. It is an advantage to have a good start of him when you see him coming.

Old Rover always starts barking outside our door if I'm not stirring soon after five-thirty in the morning. He's an intelligent old dog, but as ugly as sin, which, like the rest of us, he can't help or alter. A bob-tailed sheepdog, old and half-blind, he wouldn't stand much chance in a beauty show, while his hair is matted in knots through his never washing himself. In everybody's opinion old Rover ought to be shot. But who's to do it? For, in spite of his ragged appearance, old Rover is an affectionate old soul, and when he puts his tousled head on your knee you forget his shaggy coat and slavering jaws and see only a pair of trustful brown eyes that stare and stare as though trying to weigh up some mighty problem that affects the life of Rover and yourself only. And so, for the want of a pennyworth of shot old Rover stays on, ugly, half-blind, too old for work, and useless as a house dog, except to give a bit of a 'woof' when anyone comes down the lane.

Me and our Lizzie took the children to chapel tonight – sometimes we go to chapel and sometimes to church, it just depends – and old Rover watched us off with a wistful look, for he likes a walk out on a Sunday evening. I told him he couldn't come, so he sat watching us go, with his hairy face thrust through the lower bars of the paddock gate. We got there in good time, and all sat up straight and proper, so that our Lizzie couldn't say we were in any way misbehaving. Some late-comers opened the door, but none of us turned to look, except our Lizzie, because it isn't proper. Well, the next thing I noticed was old Rover's ugly dial peeping at me round the pew end. There he sat, his head bowed with shame like a penitent sinner, while his bit of a tail went tap-tap-tap on the carpeted aisle. Several of them started tittering, especially when the doorkeeper tried to coax him out. But Rover wasn't having any, and I was just wondering what I ought to do about it when our Lizzie nearly stove in my ribs with her elbow. So I got up and put old Rover outside, and knew by the look on our Lizzie's face she had been mortally affronted and we should hear more of it.

Poor old Rover; he's caught it all right. It's not as though he was a clean, respectable dog, but to enter a place of worship with a face like that, well! It was a lovely summer night, with birds and flowers at their best, and poor old Rover in disgrace for imitating good Christian people.

I found life very pleasant on this farm, and with more leisure time than those hard-bitten Sheffield cow-keepers allow their men. Sometimes on Sunday I harnessed old Dick in the float and took my wife and family to that village referred to as Little Norwood. Dick was a queer horse, with strange ideas about Sunday labour, for we seldom did the twelve miles there under two hours, though I tried coaxing, whipping and letting him 'gan his own gait'. In the latter case he would stop by the wayside and eat grass, while if you whipped him he just stopped altogether. It was painful the way he jogged there, as though life was a burden. But he always made up for it coming home. Hardly had time to loaden up the kiddies before Dick jumped into the collar and came spinning home like a two-year-old. He was the craftiest old horse that ever stood between shafts, and he always came home in half the time it took to go away. Anyhow, in spite of Dick's uncharitableness, we always got in a good day amongst our friends and relations.

When the Royal Agricultural Show is within easy distance of here, the boss treats his men to a day at the Show, and thus I have visited this wonderful collection of animals and machinery at Nottingham, Harrogate, Derby and Manchester. The Royal Show is such an extensive affair that you can do no more than glance at it in one day's visit. Besides cattle and farm machinery, there is the Forestry section, where you see young saplings of every kind of tree, and follow on till you see some wonders of woodcraft and wood turning; gates, handles, wheelbarrows and fancy woodwork, planed smooth as silk. The same applies to village crafts, and you see beautiful workmanship in wrought iron. And so you come to a great tent of Empire produce, and realise what an important part agriculture plays in the world. Another tent held some wonderful work done by St Dunstan's Home for the Blind, and in another you saw wool progressing from the sheep's back to the finished cloth. At lunchtime, which is when you feel ready for it, just hang around one of the seed- or cake-merchant's stands and they pull you in to lunch. That seems to be the reason for their being at the show, and should they appear tardy at inviting you inside, just dip your hand into a bag of seed-corn and start to examine the quality. They will have you inside in a jiffy, and a splendid lunch is put before you. It is a better lunch than the one you've carried about with you, and these gentlemen would feel hurt if you refused their lunch, so why not enjoy the blessings the good Lord sends.

The day has been boiling, blazing hot. Tonight the sky is overcast, and looks like thunder. Harvest began today, and I have been setting up in the oat field until eight o'clock tonight. The crops look very promising, and as I sit cooling down before going to bed I find my surroundings very pleasant. A field of barley fronts our house, and we have marked its progress as the summer advanced, from when it first showed pale green, then shot the ears, and now it stands whitened to the harvest. Not long ago we watched a cuckoo making short hops along the hedge-top, but whether it was searching for birds' eggs or seeking a nest for its own we couldn't tell from this distance. A pair of partridges thought my neighbour's garden a fit place to bring up a brood of chicks, and progressed so far as to lay fifteen eggs when the keeper came and took possession. Sometimes a wild rabbit comes into my garden. I ought to catch it, for rabbits are a nuisance in a garden. The children were missing at bedtime; found down a rabbit hole. Having run the rabbit to earth, aided by Bunty Moss and a terrier, they were strenuously digging themselves in with pointed sticks.

I stayed three years on this farm, moving with the boss when he took a larger place – Kilton Forest Farm, Worksop – in 1930. My last year was much like the other two, so it's hardly worth repeating, as nothing more important occurred than:

'Still weeding corn in my spare time, though today I escaped to mow the lawn for the missus. Got recompensed with one bottle of beer and one bun. Tonight the squire came down the lane – it's not often we see him down here – questioned all the children for about ten minutes on their names and ages and then gave them each a penny.'

'Trilby calved in the field, and all the other cows gathered round in true matronly fashion, sniffing and moving around just like the human feminine on like occasions.'

It's a curious world, and I don't know what to make of it. The longer I live, and the harder I stare at life, the less able am I to state an opinion on it. I got wondering on chance and predestination, through seeing a chap I used to know at the pit working on a road-widening job. I passed him many mornings as I drove to town in the milk-cart, and I found that, like a lot more of my old work mates, he was on relief work, and that none of them were doing very well. And I remembered that but for certain tragic happenings I would have been on relief work, or drawing the dole, during this period of depression, and I thank my stars that I am not in any way depressed, that I find life very happy, and that Helen never lived to know unhappiness, depression and the sinking feeling of hope deferred. I have much to be thankful for; but the more I think of it, the more am I puzzled to know 'What is life?'

Fifteen

A WONDERFUL YEAR

I BEGIN THE NEW YEAR BY TAKING a log of wood into the farmhouse kitchen. This is my duty at about five-thirty every New Year's morning, and it is supposed to bring good luck to the farm during the coming year. Fortunately I am the darkest-haired person on the farm, and, for the charm to be successful, it is essential that the person who lets in the new year shall have dark hair. I find at this early hour there is no one up, except the maid and the mistletoe, and half a crown left on the kitchen table overnight leads me to the belief that I, at any rate, start the new year in luck.

The boss usually asks: 'Are you turning over a new leaf this year, 'cos it's time you did, and mixed a bit o' work in among-hand.'

I get to the cowhouse about five-thirty every morning, along with little Jim, the second cowman, roll the cows' bedding up, wash down their udders and hind-quarters, dole out their milking ration, and then, with two lads to help, we sit down to milk a matter of forty cows. At eight o'clock the milk is loaded into the float and I take it to town, which takes until about eleven o'clock. After that, I really don't know what, but I mix the ration for next day, get in the hay, help to 'muck out', and do odd jobs until three p.m., when we again start milking.

Milk-drinking has increased very much of late years, milk having almost displaced ale as the national beverage, so that the cow has now become the most important animal on a farm. This is a great change from when I was

a farmer's boy. Then the horse came easily first and the milk-cow was little
thought of, being only a means of a little pin-money for the missus. There's
some fuss over the milk business nowadays, and we are visited at intervals
by milk inspectors. It has caused a great uplift in the social status of the cow.
Each cow now has its own bowl of clean water, its own towel and hairbrush,
and on inspection day I imagine them talking something like this:

'Are my horns on straight?' asks Whitefoot of Janet, and Janet, looking
over the standing boards, replies:

'Perfectly, my dear! How do you like the curl of my left horn?'

'Too sweet for words.'

'Have you noticed Rachel's coat – shabby, isn't it?'

'A perfect fright, and full of hay-seed.'

'I don't like the way she coughs, either.'

'No. I am afraid she won't pass.'

'Sh! He's coming up this side.'

The whispering ceases, and the cows stand staring, trying to appear
indifferent, whilst the vigilant-eyed inspector examines the udders, drawing
a little squirt of milk from each teat into a tiny bottle, to be analysed
and tested for microbes and tubercular germs. So the inspection ends, and
Janet, Whitefoot, Bluebell, Daisy, Rachel and the rest lie down again and
resume their cudding.

I have been thinking about thrift, not that I am ever likely to be afflicted
that way. It's Jimmy I'm thinking of. Every spring he is on the lookout for a
little place of his own. I've known dozens of farm men like that, scratch and
scrape all the best part of their lives in the hope of one day having a little
place of their own. It's a pity, for life is too short, and everything against their
ever enjoying the fruits of their thrift. By the time they are fifty they may
have saved up enough to buy a broken-winded horse and an old 'drape', but
the process of scraping and saving has so grown into the flesh that nothing
less than a surgical operation would part them from their money.

So Jimmy goes every spring place-hunting, till it has become a painful
joke, for he never takes that little spot. The pigsty will be out of order, or

the kitchen sink is in the wrong place. Always there is some slight hitch that will prevent him making the plunge. The tragedy of it. All the little pleasures of life sacrificed to a mocking vision.

I may be wrong, but when I think of old Seth or old Judd, I am inclined to the belief that thrift can easily be more vice than virtue. Old spendthrift Seth, for instance; he would want to knock off your head when he was drunk, but he would insist on your drinking with him first, and afterwards, too, if you could stand up. Judd, too; his heart and purse were in reach of any tramp who cared to put forth his hand. But these deluded clutch-pennies, how they shrivel up if a roadster says: 'Got a chew on yer, matey?'

In my spare time I have been sharpening stakes and doing a bit of fencing. A public footpath runs across our fields, and is much trodden underfoot by hikers and courting couples. The hikers are harmless enough as a rule, but the couples lean on our fences and – down go the fences. That is why, on Mondays, I must go round mending broken fences. I never saw so much wasted affection as is displayed on our footpaths on Sunday evenings.

Today the second horseman was chain-harrowing the cow pastures, and a pleasant sight to see is a fresh-harrowed pasture, showing alternate strips of light and dark green, like a mantle spread over the field.

Bluebell calved today – heifer calf. Bluebell is a dainty little Welsh heifer, with dark eyes and an inquisitive nose that is always sniffing at your sleeve in a friendly sort of way. But she is as timid as a mouse; the least false move or rustle of a straw when milking, and her foot goes in the bucket, and often the milkman goes in the gutter.

Have just returned from a do at the church institute. It was in aid of the Chinee, and as our children were in a sketch the Sunday school got up, our Lizzie took me to see them. My, but they do slate you at these church and chapel do's. I gave our Joyce sixpence to get me a cup of tea. She brought me the tea all right, and good tea it was, whether Hindoo or Chinee, but she brought me no change. I thought sixpence pretty strong, even for the best tea, and went to investigate; but the brassy-faced wench at the buffet just grinned at me, and said: 'It's for the heathen Chinee, and the vicar wants us to take all we can.'

We are bagging potatoes as though life depended on bagging potatoes. It is one of the sights of the countryside, to watch a farmer weighing a bag of potatoes, so particular is he on giving just weight. He is almost tempted to cut a potato in two to make his balance true. Bill is feeding the riddle, while Jim weighs off and ties up the bags. Jack sorts out the diseased as they pass over the riddle, and empties the seed. They find life very pleasant without the boss's company, and when he comes, saying, 'You're not getting on very fa!' they just grin and keep on turning. I say 'we' are bagging potatoes, because 'we' sounds better. In point of fact, I am busy whitewashing the cowsheds, to comply with the milk and dairies order by the sanitary inspector.

Tonight I have sown a few carrots and a row of peas. Something will have to be done about our children. They are not brought up 'becoming' like I was, and tonight our Lizzie showed me this bit of paper that one of 'em had written:

What time the buds begin to shoot
And sweeps find ready sale for soot
Poor father bends with chin to boot, and rakes.

This afternoon the boss took me to a farm near Gainsboro', where a farmer was demonstrating on how to coax a cow to part with seven or eight gallons of milk per day. It was no theoretical doctrine, for he had as fine a herd of Friesian cattle as anyone need wish for, with an average of fifteen hundred gallons per year from fifteen cows. Some agricultural college was giving a free lecture on the merits of British Friesians, balanced rations, and the capacity of a cow's rumen. It was all very interesting; as was also the lunch tent, given on the same free terms. I left the lecture for a minute or two and found the tent. There was bottled beer, tea, and ham-sandwiches. I had tea and ham-sandwiches and went back again to the lecture, feeling fortified for anything. The lecturer was stressing the necessity of a balanced ration, so after his discourse ended I hastened back to the tent and took a bottled beer to make sure my ration was properly balanced.

The long-needed rain has come, and in the fields everything looks fresh and new-washed. Yesterday it rained all day, making it a cleaning-up day. Cob-webbing, whitewashing, oiling harness and mending corn sacks were the main items, excepting when the spouts gurgled over and sparrows' nests had to be dislodged, and bubbling grates had to be liberated, because no one ever notices these obstructions until the rain comes. I noticed, as I drove home with the milk-cart, gorgeous arrays of geraniums, fuchsias, and Scarboro' lilies placed on cottage doorsteps to share in the welcome rain.

Today we are striking sugar beet, which have sprung up overnight after the storm. A thunder shower, coming of a sudden, drove us under the shelter of the hedge. It was pleasant, watching the rain making bubbles on the headland and running in little rivers in the deep-rutted cart-track. It dashed the elderflowers and ran off in a curtain of rainbow-coloured beads around our hiding place, and stirred up a rich smell of elderflowers, hemlock, and dog-roses. It was delicious, a growing day, warm and wet, so that you felt like stripping and letting the welcome rain cool your skin. After about half an hour the sun came out, and the storm passed, leaving the land all steamy and wet. We got back to our hoeing, leaving our coats and mackintoshes on the row ends in case of another sudden run, and listened to old Shep's reminiscences of bygone floods that have become village history. There's nothing spreads like a flood, except the telling of it. Floods in rivers, becks and backyards, of drowned chickens and floating pigs, of cattle rescued, and sheep carried down the river. All these, and more, make a pleasant topic of conversation as we strike, strike, strike at our sugar-beet plants.

I joined the public library this spring, one of the great benefits of living close to town. I have got through some good reading this summer, and hope to do still more. Sometimes me and Lizzie go hunting round the second-hand bookstalls, and some good books have been picked up in this way. We both like good books, and often on wet nights I read aloud to the kiddies, and from amongst these threep'ny dog-eared derelicts I have read to them bits of *Black Beauty, John Halifax, Gentleman,* Voltaire's *Zadig,* and *Timon of Athens.*

Pea-pulling is quite an event on the farms around here, and the pullers come in shoals from the colliery villages as early as four o'clock in the morning. The road is alive with their tramp, tramp, and the chatter of collier wives and wenches bent on pea-pulling. They come on foot and by cycle, they come by push-cart and by perambulator. They come on motorcycles, and they come on crutches. They come by hundreds, and for four solid hours they keep on coming. Not half of them are wanted, and not until a bobby has been called can the unwanted half be persuaded to stop pea-pulling.

They are accused of robbing the pea-field, and several bags of peas are found hidden about their person, besides in buckets, baskets, Russian boots, prams, pockets, etc.

But those that stay – the hedge becomes lined with coats, lunch baskets, cycles, and various types of wheeled carriages for infants. There are mothers who have to leave off from pea-pulling to suckle infants, and mothers who leave off just to slap them. There are girls who leave off occasionally to apply aids to beauty, and youths who leave off for good and all on account of backache. It is a busy scene while it lasts, and in these hard times makes a welcome addition to the collier's budget. The pay is from ninepence to one shilling and sixpence per bag, according to the beginning or ending of the season, and a family of them can easily make a pound per day. It is an early morning job, lasting until about noon, when the peas have to be sent straight off to Covent Garden, or some other large city market.

It is Christmas Eve. I have been on my annual pilgrimage round the shops with the kiddies. We came home laden with presents for everyone, not forgetting ourselves. They are now in bed, and me and our Lizzie have just been stocking-filling, hoping and expecting they were fast asleep. It is just a make-believe, for, though they lay still and snug, I could swear there was at least a flicker of an eyelid, and they looked altogether too innocent for my liking.

Well, now Lizzie's gone to bed, and I can sit down to write. It's nearly Christmas morning; but, before I go to bed, let me look back on this wonderful year and jot down a few words. Tomorrow we shall dine off a lump of sirloin, the boss's usual Christmas gift to his men; and sometime tomorrow I shall read some of Dickens's *Christmas Carol* to my family – they insist on my keeping up a custom I started some years ago. Many people would call it a very quiet Christmas, but, like old Scrooge, I say 'let me keep Christmas in my own way', with a few nuts, crackers, games and carols.

I said 'this wonderful year', because during the summer we had the most interesting experience that has ever happened in my life. It happened like this. We had an endowment policy mature – I think that's what they called it – and instead of putting it by for a coffin at some future date, I said to our Lizzie: 'What about a bit of a flutter? We've been in double harness a long time now, and never been away on our own, so what about going somewhere?'

She took some persuading to leave the kiddies, but we've good neighbours to keep an eye on them, and the eldest are nearly grown up, so we went. Where? London! Even now I can hardly believe it true. I had always wanted to see Westminster Abbey and St Paul's, and all the famous statues and public buildings that I had often heard talk of. And so me and our Lizzie had a week in London.

It would take another chapter to describe our visit to London; and as everybody of any account has been there themselves, why, it wouldn't interest you to wade through my chapter on London. And so I'll end by explaining how I came to write this story.

In January 1935 I was persuaded to join the Workers' Education Association, and life became fuller and richer than ever. I have studied literature mostly, being my favourite subject, but have also attended classes on Appreciation of Music, Psychology and Economics. Here let me add how grateful I am, and how life has been enlarged through the good work of the W.E.A.

The tutor of the literature class liked my written work, and he encouraged me to send some of my efforts to magazine editors. Poor editors! I have caused dozens of them to 'regret'. And then our Lizzie said: 'Why not try writing a book? Lots of folk get their lives into print nowadays, so why not a farm labourer?'

I thought a bit, and I thought a bit; for I couldn't see how anyone would be interested in a farmer joskin, and then I settled down in my spare time to write my story. And this is it. I hope you like it.

Please contact Little Toller Books
to join our mailing list or for more information
on current and forthcoming titles.

Nature Classics Library

IN THE COUNTRY *Kenneth Allsop*
THE JOURNAL OF A DISAPPOINTED MAN *W.N.P. Barbellion*
DOWN THE RIVER *H.E. Bates*
THROUGH THE WOODS *H.E. Bates*
APPLE ACRE *Adrian Bell*
MEN AND THE FIELDS *Adrian Bell*
THE MILITARY ORCHID *Jocelyn Brooke*
THE MIRROR OF THE SEA *Joseph Conrad*
ISLAND YEARS, ISLAND FARM *Frank Fraser Darling*
THE PATTERN UNDER THE PLOUGH *George Ewart Evans*
A TIME FROM THE WORLD *Rowena Farre*
SWEET THAMES RUN SOFTLY *Robert Gibbings*
THE MAKING OF THE ENGLISH LANDSCAPE *W.G. Hoskins*
A SHEPHERD'S LIFE *W.H. Hudson*
WILD LIFE IN A SOUTHERN COUNTY *Richard Jefferies*
BROTHER TO THE OX *Fred Kitchen*
FOUR HEDGES *Clare Leighton*
LETTERS FROM SKOKHOLM *R.M. Lockley*
HOME COUNTRY *Richard Mabey*
THE UNOFFICIAL COUNTRYSIDE *Richard Mabey*
RING OF BRIGHT WATER *Gavin Maxwell*
FRESH WOODS, PASTURES NEW *Ian Niall*
EARTH MEMORIES *Llewelyn Powys*
THE SOUTH COUNTRY *Edward Thomas*
THE NATURAL HISTORY OF SELBORNE *Gilbert White*
THE SHINING LEVELS *John Wyatt*

LITTLE TOLLER BOOKS
Lower Dairy Toller Fratrum Dorset DT2 OEL

Telephone: 01300 321536
books@littletoller.co.uk
www.littletoller.co.uk